When Businesses
Cross
International
Borders

THE WASHINGTON PAPERS

... intended to meet the need for an authoritative, yet prompt, public appraisal of the major developments in world affairs.

President, CSIS: David M. Abshire

Series Editor: Walter Laqueur

Director of Publications: Nancy B. Eddy

Managing Editor: Donna R. Spitler

Associate Editor: Yoma Ullman

MANUSCRIPT SUBMISSION

The Washington Papers and Praeger Publishers welcome inquiries concerning manuscript submissions. Please include with your inquiry a curriculum vitae, synopsis, table of contents, and estimated manuscript length. Manuscript length must fall between 120 and 200 double-spaced typed pages. All submissions will be peer reviewed. Submissions to *The Washington Papers* should be sent to *The Washington Papers*; The Center for Strategic and International Studies; 1800 K Street NW; Suite 400; Washington, DC 20006. Book proposals should be sent to Praeger Publishers; 90 Post Road West; P.O. Box 5007; Westport, CT 06881.

When Businesses Cross International Borders

Strategic Alliances and Their Alternatives

Harvey S. James, Jr.
Murray Weidenbaum

Foreword by John Yochelson

Published with the Center for
Strategic and International Studies
Washington, D.C.

PRAEGER

Westport, Connecticut
London

338.88
J27w

Library of Congress Cataloging-in-Publication Data

James, Harvey S.
  When businesses cross international borders : strategic alliances and their alternatives / Harvey S. James, Jr., Murray Weidenbaum.
    p.   cm. – (The Washington papers ; 161)
  Includes index.
  ISBN 0-275-94577-4. – ISBN 0-275-94578-2 (pbk.)
  1. International business enterprises.   2. Strategic alliances (Business).   3. Export marketing.   4. Foreign licensing agreements.
  5. Joint ventures.   I. Weidenbaum, Murray L.   II. Title.
  III. Series.
  HD62.4.J33   1993
  338.8 – dc20   92-36013

The *Washington Papers* are written under the auspices of The Center for Strategic and International Studies (CSIS) and published with CSIS by Praeger Publishers. CSIS, as an independent research institution, does not take specific public policy positions. Accordingly, all views, positions, and conclusions expressed in the volumes of this series should be understood to be solely those of the authors.

British Library Cataloging in Publication data is available.

Library of Congress Catalog Card Number: 92-36013
ISBN: 0-275-94577-4 (cloth)
        0-275-94578-2 (paper)

First published in 1993

Praeger Publishers, 88 Post Road West, Westport, CT 06881
An imprint of Greenwood Publishing Group, Inc.

Printed in the United States of America

The paper used in this book complies with the Permanent Paper Standard issued by the National Information Standards Organization (Z39.48-1984).

10   9   8   7   6   5   4   3   2   1

Contents

Foreword

Change in the international business environment occurs incrementally. Many of the powerful forces driving competition and market integration, both regionally and globally, have been visible for quite some time. Nevertheless, the convergence of these forces during the current period of flux in global politics sets the 1990s apart as a decade of unprecedented challenge and opportunity. Four prominent features define this setting for international business.

First, the global distribution of economic power is more evenly balanced than at any time in the past half-century. An era has ended during which the sheer size and dynamism of the U.S. economy provided an unmatched base for domestic industry as well as the clear-cut market of choice for foreign producers. The European Community now provides the core of a widening regional integrated market whose output is likely to exceed that of the United States by the end of the decade. The economies of East Asia are well on their way toward economic parity and are projected to remain the world's fastest growing region. Thus, despite its importance, the U.S. home market no longer is likely to provide the advantages and worldwide leverage of years past.

Second, global competition is intensifying on all fronts.

An explosion of international options is opening up at company level. The reach of firms is being extended at an accelerated pace by technological change, the growth of worldwide capital markets, and the increasing availability of foreign partners. At the same time, the focus of market liberalization has turned regional. The removal of internal barriers in the European Community, North America, and the Pacific Rim has increased competition not only within regions but also between them.

Third, the fault line between market and nonmarket economies has faded. The failure of communism and the spread of market-oriented ideas have established a truly historic opportunity to extend the global marketplace. The almost universal acceptance of market forces as the foundation of the future economic order is a revolutionary development that promises to bring major benefits. This expansion of market forces is likely, however, to produce strains on the limited pool of world capital resources.

Fourth, the national governments that set international rules for trade and investment are being thrown increasingly on the defensive. Political power remains concentrated at the national level, yet the reach of national governments is being undercut by varying factors: the internationalization of production; increased cross-border flows of data, money, and technology; the global scale of new challenges ranging from migration to the environment; and the increasingly assertive claims of national subgroups against central authority. The loss of control that looms at the national level has already begun to create a powerful economic as well as political backlash.

Harvey James and Murray Weidenbaum have linked the underlying forces at work in the world economy with the pursuit of corporate objectives in the international marketplace. Drawing upon a wealth of data and rich anecdotal evidence, they offer an insightful and comprehensive evaluation of alternative strategies. Their analysis defines a spectrum of options from straightforward exporting through various types of strategic alliances supported by equity investment. The advantages and disadvantages of all the options are clearly and succinctly assessed.

This volume provides an invaluable road map for business practitioners, demonstrating that there is no single approach to foreign markets but rather a host of strategies that must be systematically reviewed. The analysis is no less important for the research community and students of public policy because of the connections it draws between governmental policies and private sector commercial options.

We at the Center for Strategic and International Studies are grateful to the authors for a path-breaking contribution that illuminates for us an important new area of long-term concern.

John Yochelson
Vice President, International Business
and Economics Program
Center for Strategic and International Studies

December 1992

About the Authors

Harvey S. James, Jr., is the John M. Olin Fellow at the Center for the Study of American Business and also a doctoral student in the Department of Economics at Washington University in St. Louis.

Murray Weidenbaum holds the Mallinckrodt Distinguished Professorship at Washington University, where he is also director of the Center for the Study of American Business. He serves as cochairman of the International Research Council at the Center for Strategic and International Studies. In 1981–1982, Dr. Weidenbaum was chairman of the Council of Economic Advisers under President Ronald Reagan.

Acknowledgments

The authors acknowledge the help of Kenneth Chilton, Joseph LaPalombara, Erik Peterson, Richard Scaldini, and John Yochelson, who reviewed earlier versions of the manuscript. This research was supported by a grant from the William H. Donner Foundation to the Center for the Study of American Business, Washington University.

Summary

To respond to the rising intensity of global competition, business firms are making a variety of organizational changes. The cross-border responses that companies develop to the threats and opportunities in the international economy are diverse and complex.

This volume examines in detail the different ways that companies establish a presence in overseas markets. It describes the advantages and disadvantages of various methods of operating abroad and summarizes the considerations businesses typically explore before expanding internationally.

Chapter 1 places the analysis in the context of the globalization of the world economy and the growing trend for nations to form regional trading blocs. The specific methods employed by firms operating in the international environment can be classified in four general categories: (1) marketing abroad directly, (2) establishing cooperative contractual relationships with foreign companies, (3) operating wholly owned facilities in other nations, and (4) entering into strategic alliances.

Chapter 2 describes the direct methods of entering foreign markets without actually establishing local production facilities. The two most common ways are exporting directly to the targeted markets and engaging in turnkey operations. Exporting, historically one of the most important means of acquiring an international presence, continues to be a prominent and effective strategy today.

Cooperative contractual relationships, discussed in chapter 3, are strategies employed when firms wish to gain access to foreign markets without the substantial investment of capital and other resources typically necessary in operating wholly owned facilities abroad. They are also useful when governmental policies restrict investment by foreign companies or impose barriers to foreign trade. Cooperative contractual agreements include licensing, franchising, and subcontracting.

The operation of wholly owned production and distribution facilities in foreign countries is one of the most preferred methods of gaining and maintaining a presence overseas. As described in chapter 4, firms typically employ this strategy either by building new facilities (often called greenfield operations) or by merging with or acquiring existing companies or divisions.

Strategic alliances comprise nearly every form of collaborative relationship engaged in by firms. Because so many types of alliances have evolved, a useful distinction can be made between those that involve a substantial equity investment and those that do not.

Chapter 5 describes nonequity alliances, and chapter 6 presents an analysis of equity partnerships. The nonequity forms of interfirm alliance include cooperation in research and development, technology swaps and cross-licensing agreements, joint production or marketing associations, and informal alliances.

Equity alliances consist of joint ventures, equity swaps, formal affiliations, and other forms of investment partnerships. These tend to be more enduring and ambitious projects than nonequity alliances or simple licensing arrangements, although they often evolve out of joint research projects, informal alliances, or other cooperative associations between firms.

The particular cross-border strategy adopted by a company is closely affected by the goals of the firm, as well as by the specific economic, political, and social conditions of the host country. One particularly interesting finding is that the approach used by businesses (joint venture, acquisition, licensing, et cetera) often depends on the nature of the obstacles a host government's policies place before foreign commerce. Regardless of the specific approach used, however, the globally oriented firms tend to compete more successfully in the world marketplace than companies limited to a single geographic market.

When Businesses Cross International Borders

1

Competing in a Global Marketplace

Fundamental changes are occurring in the very nature of the private business enterprise as it responds to the threats and opportunities of the global marketplace. Even the firm most oriented to domestic business is increasing its geographic reach as its suppliers and customers are, with increasing frequency, located on a variety of continents.

As the intensity of global competition increases, many companies are forced to reevaluate their niche in the world marketplace. For some companies this entails strengthening their domestic position against competing foreign products. Other firms respond by aggressively expanding their operations into foreign markets. For many, collaborative agreements with other businesses are an effective alternative to the more traditional approaches. These partnerships – which can extend to strategic alliances – may be viewed as intermediate positions between a focus on domestic markets and full-scale global operations.[1]

The modern enterprise is increasingly developing multinational networks composed of alliances, affiliates, licensees, and other partnerships. Mergers and acquisitions often involve crossing national boundaries – and dealing with two or more national governments, as well as with a variety of state, provincial, and local authorities.

Partially owned subsidiaries, associated firms, licensing, and correspondent relationships are also on the rise. Large enterprises that were once content to concentrate their production, research, and exports in their home economies are forging international ties. Often the same companies engage in joint ventures to develop new products, coproduce existing products, serve as sources of supply for each other, share output, and compete. There is no universal pattern. But, as we will show, the specific ways in which companies establish their presence in overseas markets is often strongly influenced by particular obstacles and restrictions established by the host country (and occasionally by the home country).

On the one hand, the geographic spread of business firms has exposed national enterprises to the pressures and promises of many sovereigns, making their actions less responsive to the demands of national authorities in the home country. On the other hand, the spread of the national enterprise into foreign locations can enhance the strength of the national economy, allowing it better access to foreign resources and technologies.[2]

As a consequence, various companies – in the same nation and often in the same industry – are responding to the global marketplace differently, depending on the regional markets in which they are participating or seeking to enter.

For the individual business firm, the rapid changes in the international economy offer both threat and opportunity. There is great similarity between the domestic threat of hostile takeovers and the loss of market position owing to new foreign competition. In both cases, the firm is forced to review its strengths and weaknesses and to rethink its long-term strategy. Streamlining, downsizing, accelerating product development, and organizational restructuring are often responses to both internal takeover threats and foreign competition.

One outcome of globalization is that corporate structures are changing and newer forms of business relationships are evolving. In referring to enterprises that have little formal organization at all, J. Brian Quinn of Dartmouth remarks, "We're seeing a series of really weird-looking corporate structures." He calls them "spiders' webs" held together simply by networks of communications. In other cases, companies have adopted such flat organizational structures that they may have 40 people or a dozen units reporting to just one authority.[3]

In an important sense, becoming a global company is as much a process as an objective and more a journey than a destination. One team of consultants notes the successive changes that companies experience on the road from domestic producer to regional exporter to global exporter to international operations to the truly global enterprise (see figure 1.1).[4] The global manager's task is to pace the movement along the global continuum and to gear that choice to specific times and locations.

Basic Forces in the Global Marketplace

Two conflicting trends are affecting the activities of businesses abroad – regionalization and globalization. On the most visible level, governments are entering into regional coalitions or trading blocs. The rise of the European Community (EC) and the North American Free Trade Agreement (NAFTA) are cogent examples. At a more subtle but perhaps more fundamental level, individual enterprises are learning how to expand their markets and overcome the trade and investment barriers erected by governments. This is brought home by the undramatic but powerful change taking place in the organizational composition of international trade. For advanced economies – such as Japan, the United States, and the member nations of the EC – often as much as one-half of the trade crossing their international borders consists of internal transfers within the same enterprise.

A U.S.-based corporation may furnish capital goods to a subsidiary in Europe, an Asian-based company may ship

FIGURE 1.1
Levels of Globalization

DOMESTIC	REGIONAL EXPORTER	EXPORTER	INTERNATIONAL	INTERNATIONAL TO GLOBAL	GLOBAL
Operate exclusively within a single country	Operate within a geographically defined region that crosses national boundaries. Markets served are economically and culturally homogeneous.	Run operations from a central office in the home region, exporting finished goods to a variety of countries. Some marketing outside the home region.	Regional operations are somewhat autonomous, but key decisions are coordinated from central office in the home region. Manufacturing and assembly, marketing and sales are decentralized beyond the home region.	Run independent and mainly self-sufficient subsidiaries in a range of countries. Some functions (R&D, sourcing, financing) are decentralized. The home region is still the primary base for many functions.	Highly decentralized organization operating across a broad range of countries. No geographic area is assumed to be the primary base for any functional area. Each function is performed in the most suitable location.

Source: Joseph Nemec, Jr., and Barbara A. Failer, *A Special Report on Globalization* (New York: Booz-Allen & Hamilton, 1991).

components or goods in process to a division in the United States, and a European-based corporation may ship consumer goods to its marketing subsidiary in Asia.[5]

As we shall see, business firms are responding in ways that they consider productive and profitable, subject to the political, social, and economic environments they find themselves in. One result of these two contrasting developments is that the role of the individual nation-state is diminishing.

Implications of Regionalization

The regionalization of the world economies is being formulated around three principal trading blocs, although the likelihood of a purely trilateral world economy is a subject of considerable debate. To some degree, the EC, the North American region, and the East Asian nations are each concentrating on matters internal to their respective regions rather than on global issues. Such regionalization is desirable if the elimination of national restraints permits economies of scale that promote efficiency and productivity.

Another basic result of regionalization commands far less attention, however; it is the development of more insular or inward-looking patterns of international commerce. For instance, in 1960, before the Common Market gained momentum, more than 60 percent of the foreign trade of its 12 nations was carried on outside what is now the European Community. But currently, 60 percent or more of the trade of the EC stays inside the community – a complete reversal.[6] The completion of the integration process is bound to increase that ratio further.

The rise of the Asian rim economies, under the leadership of Japan, is generating a similar trend. As in the EC, more than 60 percent of the trade of these nations stays within the area.[7] The six nations making up ASEAN, or the Association of Southeast Asian Nations (Malaysia, Indonesia, the Philippines, Thailand, Singapore, and Brunei), are now a larger market for Japan than is the United States.

Many of those "imports," however, become components of items that are ultimately exported to the EC or North America.

Given the expansion of trade and investment in both Western Europe (and probably in parts of Eastern Europe as well) and East Asia, it should not be surprising that the nations of North America have, belatedly, developed their own response. Following the U.S.-Canadian free trade agreement, a similar tripartite arrangement with Mexico — NAFTA — has been negotiated. Conceivably, this arrangement will extend to other major trading nations in the Western Hemisphere in the future.

The question then arises: On balance, will regionalization reduce or increase world trade? The data will be difficult to interpret. The continued rise in regionalization is likely to coincide with the growth in international commerce. It will not, however, be a cause and effect relationship. Another development — the globalization of business — will pace the growth of world trade.

Implications of Globalization

Many observers believe that the pressures for a more global orientation of business activities will overwhelm the trend toward regionalization during the 1990s.[8] Some of these forces include an equalization of earnings and a homogenization of tastes worldwide. Higher incomes have also given rise to international markets for national specialty products, such as Italian shoes, Swiss watches, and Japanese consumer electronics.[9] In addition, a general reduction in trade barriers began in the 1980s and has continued through the present time, especially in Latin America.[10] Still, governments continue to set up myriad restrictions on imports and foreign investment to "protect" domestic jobs.

The spark that ultimately ignited global competition, however, was the need to find new markets for mass-produced goods when existing markets became saturated in the face of rising industrial productivity.[11] In response, firms rushed to increase their presence worldwide by extending the scope of operations globally and by taking advantage of scale economies.

Political and military factors also provide impetus toward globalization and affect business operations abroad. The North Atlantic Treaty Organization (NATO) may be a smaller factor in current European decision making than in the 1980s, but great uncertainty remains as to who will control the powerful military arsenal located in the former Soviet republics. In any event, as long as Japan maintains its current constitutional barrier to nuclear forces, and the People's Republic of China (PRC) and the former Soviet republics retain their nuclear military strength, the United States and other key industrialized nations will continue to be affected by broader geopolitical concerns.

One scholar, however, sees a "diffusion of power" across the globe in the 1990s, with the great powers less able to use their traditional power resources to achieve their purposes.[12] The further advance of technology, especially in the fields of communication and transportation, will continue to reduce the importance of national borders. Technological progress makes possible a variety of business innovations that often overcome the obstacles imposed by parochial governments. As the pressures for globalization continue to increase, many nations – particularly the developing nations – will recognize the need to liberalize their trade policies and other regulations that affect business activity within their borders. Indeed, technological advance and the need to attract business activity will be far more powerful forces than governmentally imposed restrictions.

The impact of the globalization of economic competition has been profound. Quality, variety, customization, convenience, and timely delivery of state-of-the-art products and services often become the competitive edge.[13] Some analysts contend that the further globalization of companies is leading to their effective denationalization.

Likewise, the distinction between foreign and domestic products is increasingly blurred.

A more extreme position views the joint ventures involving larger multinational firms as "corporate galaxies," in which the dominant firms are linked to a number of smaller national companies. Even from this viewpoint, the competitive process is still at work—but its focus has grown from domestic to regional to global markets.[14]

In the years ahead, the combined power of economic incentives and technological change will increasingly compel consumers and government officials to wake up to the positive implications of the global economy. Nevertheless, the real liberalization of trade will arise, not from liberating actions by government, but from the power of competition among business firms in the private sector.

Establishing an Overseas Business Presence

As the following chapters of this book will show, U.S. businesses are operating in the world marketplace in numerous ways. Exporting continues to be important for most firms participating in the international economy. Exports, however, can be slowed down by tariffs and quotas. Licensing also has drawbacks because licenses can be abused by licensees who violate the quality control provisions of the license or who sell in markets not covered by the license. Experienced enterprises, therefore, tend to establish their positions in foreign markets through subsidiaries in preference to, or at least in addition to, exports and independent licensees.

When the foreign subsidiary approach proves inadequate to provide the required linkage to foreign markets, technology, and capital, large firms also resort to various types of alliances with foreign firms, often including potential competitors.[15] The financial demands of developing and producing a new generation of high-technology products—

whether a jet airliner or a computer system – are so awesome that the largest company can rarely proceed on its own.

Indeed, there are many types of interfirm cooperation. Technological agreements are traditional. Licensing provides access to technical shortcuts and makes it possible to catch up or diversify. (This type of cooperation can also develop into a two-way exchange of know-how and joint research.) Commercial and financial cooperation makes it possible to extend and globalize distribution networks.

Each of these approaches to cross-border cooperation among business firms has its unique set of advantages and disadvantages. Some of these mechanisms are appropriate to competitive markets, others to economies where government influence is great. Some are appropriate to the design and production of goods, others to the service sectors. The sections that follow will focus on four major alternative ways in which businesses can penetrate international markets: (1) direct exporting, (2) licensing and franchising products and services, (3) establishing overseas production facilities and acquiring foreign firms, and (4) entering into joint ventures and affiliate and correspondent relationships. Often the same firm will use two or more of the available alternatives, depending on its needs and the possibilities and restrictions in the host country.

Methods of Penetrating International Markets

Direct Exporting

The oldest strategy for cross-border business activity is directly exporting from the home country. The advantages of exporting are fundamental: it enables the company to expand its markets beyond traditional domestic customers while maintaining full control of product quality.

The ability to export is one of the primary outward

manifestations of the global competitiveness of a firm. This is especially true as many businesses that previously enjoyed a stable and profitable domestic presence are forced into the international marketplace by competing foreign companies that are penetrating their home markets. In marketing abroad, the firm competes from its domestic location, generally without the immediate involvement of foreign enterprises. Thus, the company's home base remains the primary location for the design, production, and distribution of its products. It may interact with foreign companies. Indeed, the direct marketing of a firm's products or services may involve the creation of close business ties with foreign importers. The primary responsibility of decision making and production, however, rests with the domestic enterprise.

Licensing and Franchising Overseas

For a variety of reasons, many companies want to establish an overseas presence with a minimum of investment and risk, either because of their financial restraints or their fear of the unknown. At other times, governmental obstacles restrict or prevent direct exports or full ownership of a business in a specific country. In either of these circumstances, manufacturing companies can license their products for production and sale by foreign firms. Likewise, service firms can franchise their type of operations to overseas companies.

Producing Abroad

For a variety of economic and political reasons, many companies exporting on a large scale also produce overseas. Establishing a foreign manufacturing facility economizes on transportation costs and readily enables the company to make items tailored to local consumer preferences. Moreover, the overseas locations often serve as a means of surmounting governmental barriers to imports.

Acquiring Foreign Firms

At times, the fastest way of penetrating a foreign market is to buy out a company already doing business in that country. This approach avoids the time and trouble it takes to start an enterprise from scratch. Integrating an acquired firm is not easy, however, even if both companies are located in the same country. Coordinating across national borders presents added difficulties ranging from differences in language and culture to governmental requirements and restrictions. The ease of modern communication and transportation surely helps on this score.

Because this method of penetrating foreign markets often encounters all sorts of political and regulatory restrictions, firms headquartered in advanced industrial nations frequently share ownership with local investors.

Joint Ventures and Other
Cooperative Relationships

Many companies increasingly understand the significance of a growing world marketplace. They realize that exporting and establishing overseas operations are no longer the only choices they have in participating in international markets. Cooperation with businesses abroad is becoming significantly evident as an alternative response. The mechanisms involved include contractual agreements between firms as well as more intricate partnerships that comprise various forms of alliances and affiliations.

The term "strategic alliance" has become a catchall phrase comprising nearly every form of collaborative relationship a firm may enter into. Companies may be linked in all sorts of ways without being involved in an alliance, including taking on such long-term relationships as becoming customers or suppliers. In an alliance, both companies share some risk in the investments they have made, financially or otherwise, in the common activity.

The most rapidly changing route for large companies

entering overseas markets is through a growing variety of joint ventures and strategic alliances. These range from research and development (R&D) cooperatives and technology swaps to joint production and marketing agreements to joint equity swaps. The common characteristic of these actions is that two or more companies, often located on different continents, enter into relatively long-lasting joint endeavors.

Strategic alliances are set up in so many combinations and permutations that it is difficult, and often misleading, to generalize. Nevertheless, we will try to do just that in this book. Acknowledging the many gray areas, we find it useful to divide strategic alliances into two categories: those that involve a substantial equity investment in new undertakings and those that do not.[16]

The nonequity style of intercorporate alliances includes cooperation on new R&D as well as interchange of existing technology. The more informal alliances include agreements to produce cooperatively or to market cooperatively (or both).

Research and development and technology-swapping alliances are special forms of strategic alliances in which firms cooperate on the basic design of proprietary technologies or production processes. Some of these alliances typically evolve into other partnerships, such as the joint production and marketing of products developed together. In the latter case, the basis of the cooperation usually continues to be the development and sharing of mutually beneficial technologies.

Joint production and marketing agreements are similar in nature to R&D cooperation but are centered around the production and distribution phases of the product cycle. As is typical with many strategic alliances, however, firms engaging in joint production or marketing arrangements have also cooperated closely in R&D or in other activities. Thus, joint production and joint marketing activities are often another aspect of a more extensive strategic alliance among companies.

Strategic alliances involving equity investments by each of the partners tend to be more ambitious and often more enduring undertakings. Moreover, firms undertaking equity-investment alliances usually have a specific purpose or objective in mind for the partnership. At the heart of the arrangement is typically a joint venture, to which each of the partners has committed money, personnel, and other corporate resources. The agreement may also cover other types of arrangements, notably the interchange of technology and the supplying or purchasing of each other's products.

Compared to establishing wholly owned enterprises, strategic alliances may involve more modest investments — although significantly in excess of those for such other strategies as exporting or licensing. Their other characteristics also fall "in between" these two alternatives, as does the degree of risk, the profit potential, and the degree of control over the resultant products and their manufacturing and sales.

Some alliances consist of simple cross-border partnerships, in which the company participates in the foreign market with a local firm. Other alliances are true global ventures, in which multinational corporations cooperate with other global firms at several levels of the organization and in multiple locations, usually with the objective of expanding the operations of both firms on a worldwide level.

Business Responses to Government

Many business decisions are responses to specific policy actions by government. In an open economy, companies in one nation freely export to and import from firms in other nations, influenced primarily by the comparative advantage offered by the physical and human resources available in the different trading nations. Indeed, despite the many barriers erected by government, commerce between nations remains very substantial and continues to grow significantly.

For a variety of political reasons — mainly to "protect"

home industry owners, managers, and employees, but sometimes on ostensible national security grounds – governments often place barriers to international trade. The most notable are tariffs, quotas, domestic content restrictions, and reciprocity rules. Foreign-based companies can respond in a variety of ways: absorbing the increased costs, establishing manufacturing operations in the target country, or acquiring a local firm – or forgoing that market.

In the case of quotas, exporting firms can and do shift to higher priced items, on which the unit profits are higher. Thus they can try to maintain their overall earnings. Where companies try to sell goods directly to foreign governments (notably military equipment), they often have to share the contract with local enterprises, either by subcontracting or purchasing locally or developing the product jointly.

Firms doing business in other nations also confront a variety of investment barriers. Especially in the case of developing nations, the host government often limits the degree of foreign ownership in any local enterprise. "Foreign" firms frequently respond by entering into joint ventures with local companies, or, in extreme cases, literally giving away nominal majority ownership.

Other ways around investment barriers include, in the case of manufactured goods, entering into agreements with local firms that will produce the item under licensing arrangements. In the case of services, franchising serves a similar purpose. When faced with the threat of expropriation or restrictions on repatriation of earnings, large, well-established foreign companies set up affiliates or correspondent relationships with local firms.

The barriers to international commerce may be in the area of taxes and regulations or be informal in nature. When a foreign government establishes onerous tax and regulatory structures, the multinational firm may have the option of shifting its high value-added activities to nations with more benign tax and regulatory regimes. Where the high taxes and regulations are imposed by the home country, the firm has an added incentive to shift production overseas, using one or more of the mechanisms just described.

In the case of informal barriers—such as in nations whose traditions tend to favor established companies over newcomers—the standard response by the foreign firm is often to market through local distributors. A great many Western companies that have succeeded in winning large shares of the Japanese market, for example, have done so through establishing long-term relationships with local distributors.

It should be emphasized that traditional business reasons are also involved in the choice among the available methods of penetrating foreign markets. Indeed, those business concerns may often be the dominating influence.

From the viewpoint of the U.S. firm, the various types of cross-border, cross-company arrangements represent a new level of decision making, which has traditionally been ignored by businesses satisfied with serving a large, growing continent-wide domestic market. There is also another side to the coin of overseas market penetration. Even as domestic companies are engaged in interfirm cooperation in an effort to penetrate foreign markets, many foreign enterprises are trying to turn the tables on them by penetrating their home markets.

The contemporary international marketplace offers many possibilities for individual economic units to operate strategically. Yet few firms fully meet the ideal, and a great many do not even try. Nevertheless, the pace of business activity is increasingly being set by the more global firm.

2

Marketing Abroad Directly

The presence of an emerging worldwide market underscores the necessity for firms to develop strategies that will enable them to compete successfully on a global scale. Although many strategies are available for firms to pursue — cooperative contractual relationships, strategic alliances and joint ventures, and the establishment or acquisition of overseas production facilities — the need for globally oriented firms to get their products into foreign markets is paramount.

For many firms, selling products directly to foreign markets represents a practical and attractive response. This is especially true for small or mid-size companies faced with competition in their domestic markets by foreign businesses and possessing limited financial resources for full-scale global operations.

There are primarily two ways in which an established firm can directly market its products in foreign nations without setting up local production facilities or strategic relationships with foreign businesses: exporting and turnkey operations. Exporting involves the transfer of goods from the firm's domestic production facilities to foreign customers. Turnkey operations, on the other hand, typically consist of the construction of plants by the domestic firm in the foreign country and are often accompanied by the direct exportation of capital equipment.

Exporting

Traditionally, exporting refers to the transfer of domestically produced products to customers in foreign countries. The nature of exporting has been changing considerably in recent years, however, because of the increased globalization of the world's economy. Thus, exporting can include both the shipment of goods from domestic sources to foreigners as well as sales from a firm's foreign subsidiary to domestic customers. We will refer here primarily to transfers from the domestic source to foreigners.

Most firms engaged in foreign trade, especially small and medium-size companies, export their products or services directly to foreign customers. Yet, in some circumstances, businesses may use the services of an international trading company, especially in attempting to penetrate the Japanese market. It is intriguing to note that many formal complaints filed with Japan's governmental ombudsman come from Japanese trading companies trying to export from the United States.[1]

Because U.S. firms do business with every other nation in the world, it is useful to see where the major trade flows go. In 1991, approximately one-half of U.S. exports were bought by companies in five nations: Canada, Japan, Mexico, the United Kingdom, and Germany (in that order). To add five other countries – South Korea, France, Taiwan, Singapore, and Italy – accounts for nearly two-thirds of U.S. export markets (see table 2.1). The same ten nations are the source for more than two-thirds of the imports into the United States, although the individual national rankings differ between imports and exports.

Although the United States has a large, albeit declining, trade deficit, it is not so apparent that U.S. firms are

TABLE 2.1
Major U.S. Trading Partners, Based on 1991 Trade Flows

Country	Exports		Imports	
	U.S. $billions	Percent	U.S. $billions	Percent
Canada	85.1	20.2	91.1	18.7
Japan	48.1	11.4	91.6	18.8
Mexico	33.3	7.9	31.2	6.4
United Kingdom	22.1	5.2	18.5	3.8
Germany	21.3	5.0	26.2	5.4
South Korea	15.5	3.7	17.0	3.5
France	15.4	3.7	13.4	2.7
Taiwan	13.2	3.1	23.0	4.7
Singapore	8.8	2.1	10.0	2.0
Italy	8.6	2.0	11.8	2.4
Subtotal	271.4	64.3	333.8	68.4
All other	150.5	35.7	154.3	31.6
Total	421.9	100.0	488.1	100.0

Source: U.S. Department of Commerce.

necessarily less competitive than their foreign counterparts across the board. High-tech companies in the United States have consistently maintained a favorable trade balance, although low-tech companies have suffered most severely from foreign competition.[2] During the 1980s, U.S. trade surpluses in advanced-technology products have averaged over $20 billion a year. In 1991 alone, U.S. firms exported $37 billion more advanced-technology products than they imported, further illustrating the fact that U.S. high-tech companies enjoy a considerable, although not guaranteed, competitive advantage.[3] Thus, even in the face of severe foreign competition, exporting remains a significant strategic response for many firms.

Among the larger firms – those with more than 10,000 employees – almost 60 percent expect their exports to increase, compared with 41 percent of firms with fewer than 100 employees.[4] Moreover, among the member companies of the American Business Conference (ABC), exporting accounted for more than one-half of all strategies for entering foreign countries.[5] This suggests that exporting is a vital part of operations, at least for many large enterprises.

Among the three major North American countries (the United States, Canada, and Mexico), the closer commercial links fostered over the years will ensure that exporting strategies (among others) continue to be important for U.S. businesses. Progressive reduction in tariff barriers during the 1980s has been a positive force. In 1982, the average duty on imports to Mexico was in excess of 27 percent; in the case of Canada, the average rate was about 14 percent. In comparison, typical tariffs levied by the United States came to less than 5 percent. By 1989, the Mexican trade barriers had declined to the neighborhood of 14 percent and the Canadian rate averaged about 11 percent. U.S. tariffs remained below 5 percent.[6]

Large corporations are not alone in employing exporting as a strategic response. Many small and mid-size companies are finding that exporting is becoming increasingly essential as a marketing strategy, especially in the face of severe domestic competition from foreign products. For example, Southern Gold Honey Company, a small producer of honey in Texas for more than 15 years, saw its domestic sales fall considerably as consumers at home purchased less expensive imported honey. Although the company lost considerable market share in the United States, it was able to locate importers in the Middle East, which resulted in a quadrupling of sales.[7]

Although exporting represents a significant strategy for numerous firms, engaging in foreign trade is often part of a much larger global strategy. Many companies have become more globally oriented by progressing from simple trade with a foreign nation to the development of wholly owned production facilities, joint ventures, or other cooperative partnerships with foreign companies.[8] This is because a successful exporting operation, by definition, requires firms to develop effective business links with foreign firms. These associations are often the precursors of more extensive cooperative relationships or strategic alliances with overseas companies.[9]

An illustration of how exporting may lead to a more comprehensive global strategy is the history of Pall Corporation, a producer of specialized filtration equipment. Pall began building its 30-year international presence by first exporting from the United States to the United Kingdom. When it was approached by a Japanese importer who suggested the company's product would sell well in Asian markets, the company also began selling its products in Japan. Later, the company acquired a related English firm and eventually incorporated the Japanese distributor as a Pall subsidiary.[10]

Pall penetrated the sophisticated French market for wine filters by designing a new French version of its filters. The company then went on to enter the Italian wine market with a third variation of its product.

In some countries, exporting is being facilitated by the formation of joint business ventures among firms. These ventures, known as export cartels, are used as a way to limit risks and save money as companies seek to learn more about foreign markets from firms within the same industry. For smaller firms, such as catfish farmers, flour millers, and textile manufacturers, these cartels are the only effective means of gaining access to foreign markets. Furthermore, in the United States, firms participating in the cartels for the purpose of exporting are given virtual antitrust immunity by the Commerce Department, which allows them to trade market and price information so long as the practice does not significantly affect competition within the United States.[11]

Advantages

The principal advantage of exporting is that it allows the firm to earn additional income and profits by selling its products in more than one market. Similarly, by exporting, firms may also be able to broaden market risks and reduce the effects of downturns in the domestic market. This is particularly important for a company that is finding its domestic market share reduced by price and quality competition from foreign products.[12]

For Marsh-McBirney, a manufacturer of sewage system flow meters, exports in 1990 accounted for approximately 15 percent of total sales, nearly double the rate from a decade earlier and twice the industry norm. Thus, when domestic sales fell as a result of the 1990–1991 recession, Marsh-McBirney was able to focus more attention on sales abroad, which allowed the company to maintain production levels.[13]

By marketing products directly from the domestic production site, a firm is also able to maintain a far higher degree of control over research, design, or production decisions than if facilities were located at several sites around the world, or if the firm were involved in a form of strategic affiliation with foreign companies. The preservation of tight control over research and production decisions may be necessary to safeguard sensitive technologies or encourage a fast product development cycle.

Moreover, direct marketing strategies allow the firm to maintain domestic production facilities or continue to employ domestic resources, even when its primary customers are located in foreign countries. For example, even though the foreign airline market is growing much faster than its domestic counterpart, the major U.S. producers – Boeing and McDonnell Douglas – continue to export from a domestic R&D and product development base. In the case of aircraft production, with sharply declining marginal costs, it is extremely expensive to start up secondary production sites, especially in overseas locations.

Disadvantages

A fundamental disadvantage of exporting is that firms must deal with foreign barriers to entry, such as tariffs and quotas. A related problem concerns local content laws that require that a certain percentage of an imported good be made in the targeted country.

Furthermore, uncertain fluctuations in exchange rates may make operating from a domestic position risky. For instance, exports often decline when the home currency rises against foreign currencies; domestic goods become more expensive relative to goods produced abroad. U.S. firms may be able to overcome these risks by pricing in dollars or selling to countries in which exchange rates with the United States are relatively stable, such as Canada.[14] Nevertheless, these and similar strategies may severely restrict the number of potential markets in which a firm can sell its products, especially because relatively few of the many world currencies are convertible to U.S. dollars in the open market.[15]

Another disadvantage of exporting is that some firms may find it difficult or expensive to locate and maintain a successful relationship with foreign importers. Furthermore, determining how to distribute products in foreign markets presents a big challenge, particularly for small or medium-size firms. For instance, Avid Technologies of Burlington, Massachusetts, a maker of a computer system that edits film and videotape, allows foreign distributors to keep up to 40 percent of the revenue.[16] For some firms this approach offers the only way to gain access to foreign markets, but many other companies may consider it too steep a price to pay.

Another disadvantage of exporting is the added expense associated with shipping products to other countries, such as high transportation costs (for example, for cement) and the need to overcome barriers to trade. Trade barriers may range from simple quotas on the quantity that can be imported, such as motor vehicles, textiles, and agricultural products, to the outright prohibition of particular imported products, such as Brazil's ban on imported computer equipment. In fact, 45 percent of U.S. firms in a 1991 survey reported that "trade barriers imposed by other countries" presented the greatest impediment to selling abroad.[17]

Indirect barriers, such as inadequate patent protection laws, may also impede a firm's ability to market its products successfully in a foreign country. Marsh-McBirney reports that the company is especially hurt by the weakness of patent protection overseas. In particular, company officials believe that its export business in Europe would double if its patented products were adequately protected there.[18]

The Decision to Export

For many companies with little experience in trading across borders, the decision of exactly how to go about marketing abroad is often very difficult to make.

Reasons to Export. Exporting is an effective strategy when there are significant scale economies within the production process, or when a steep learning curve makes it advantageous to remain in one location. For instance, firms in traditional export-based industries, such as aircraft, machinery, materials, and agriculturally related products, have long operated from one primary location in the United States.[19]

Exporting is effective when the company is able to locate an overseas market niche that it is able to exploit from its domestic location. Paul Newman's Own Spaghetti Sauce sells well in Finland, a country traditionally not responsive to imported tomato products. The company found a particular market niche – Finns like American products and empty ships run regularly from the United States to Finland.[20]

Similarly, exporting may be appropriate when a firm is able to produce a better product at home than its competitors do abroad. For example, Rad Elec, a small company based in Maryland, sells radon test kits that are technologically superior to the conventional kits because, unlike the others, they produce readings at the site. Consequently, Rad Elec's products sell well not only in the United States but also in Sweden and Canada.[21]

Reasons Not to Export. As indicated earlier, strategies other than exporting are typically more effective when substantial foreign barriers to trade exist or when international economic conditions are uncertain—for example, when sharply varying exchange rates make the returns from exporting unpredictable.

The case of the economic integration of the EC is illustrative. Trade within the EC is being significantly promoted, but the trade wall around the EC is not coming down. In fact, the EC has been toughening its external barriers to commerce. For example, the French government has announced new restrictions on TV programming from the United States (one of the few favorable items in the U.S. balance of trade). To "promote" EC-wide TV programming, the French are limiting non-EC programming to 40 percent of total air time. (As we will show later, many U.S. companies have overcome EC trade barriers by acquiring local firms.)

Moreover, exporting is generally not appropriate when there are high transportation, communication, or storage costs that make production in one central location inefficient.[22] Under these circumstances, dispersing the production activities among several nations can be a more effective strategy.

This is also true when consumer preferences differ across countries. For instance, when the costs of modifying the home market product to meet local tastes or regulatory requirements are excessive, the exporting firm may find it better to localize production by direct foreign investment or some other strategy.[23] Many firms have found ways around this, however, by changing the nature of the products they export.

Plumley, a manufacturer of auto engine hoses, tried to export directly to its European customers. Because each required a different fit or type of metal coupling, Plumley found it necessary to locate a German-based partner to make the fittings and handle sales to its European clients. Now Plumley exports bare hoses in bulk to the German company, thus avoiding the cost and delay of refitting for different customers.[24]

For firms in some industries, exporting may not be a particularly feasible option. Roughly 60 percent of U.S. manufacturers export, while approximately 10 percent of transportation/utilities, 8 percent of finance and wholesale/retail, and less than 5 percent of service and construction firms sell abroad.[25]

Turnkey Operations

Turnkey operations are projects in which a company designs, constructs, and installs capital equipment with the intention of turning over control and operation to the purchasers.[26] Turnkey operations are important in a number of different industries, most notably the construction of electric utility plants and other large-scale capital works. Other examples include the construction of food processing or food packaging plants, water conservation and pollution-control systems, transportation, and telecommunication systems.

Turnkey projects are not necessarily confined to the construction of large-scale facilities, however. Many firms sell or fabricate a unique system of specialized equipment with the intent of turning over its operation to the purchaser. Novatec, a Baltimore-based company, installed the material-handling and drying system at General Motors' Saturn plant in Spring Hill, Tennessee. The operation of the equipment was left to Saturn engineers.[27] Similarly, Capsule Technology Group, a Canadian manufacturer and marketer of gelatin drug capsules, engages in turnkey projects by building and installing capsule-making machinery for other companies around the world.[28]

Turnkey operations differ from other forms of contractual business relationships, such as subcontracting the production or assembly of components to other companies, in that the supplier takes responsibility for all aspects of the design and construction of the equipment. Thus, although other companies may be used to assist in the development or assembly of key subsystems, the primary supplier remains heavily involved in all aspects of the project.

One of the primary motivations for engaging in turnkey operations is that, like subcontracting or licensing agreements, they allow firms access to markets overseas that would otherwise reject a foreign manufacturing presence. Once the project is completed, however, the supplying firm has no control over the use of the facility or the marketing of the product produced.

During the 1960s, Fiat built automobile-producing plants in Poland and the former USSR instead of selling automobiles directly to those countries. Although a second generation of cars was derived from Fiat technology, Fiat had no control over their production and sale once the original agreement had expired.[29]

The Decision to Establish Turnkey Operations

For the most part, firms heavily involved in turnkey operations represent a specialized group of producers. Consequently, the decision to engage in turnkey operations is intrinsically associated with the nature of a firm's product.

Nevertheless, some firms may have alternatives to establishing turnkey operations, such as subcontracting or operating the assembled plant as a wholly owned or jointly owned subsidiary. The key to deciding on the ownership structure depends closely on the political climate and the nature of governmental regulations in the country in which the processing plant is constructed.

Conclusion

The direct approach to competing in a global economy via exporting from the home country remains an important strategy for most companies involved in business beyond their borders. The nature of maintaining a home base and exporting from it has, however, been changing during the past two decades. For example, while U.S. exports have risen steadily during this period, the share of world trade accounted for by all U.S. companies has remained relatively constant at around 17 percent. U.S. firms are exporting less from the United States and more from their production facilities in other countries.[30] This illustrates the increasingly complex nature of exporting in a global marketplace and its relationship to other strategies. In the chapters that follow, we examine these other strategies.

3

Cooperative Contractual Arrangements

Cooperative contractual agreements are business relationships in which a domestic firm gains access to global markets without making the large financial or technical investments often required to establish exporting links or wholly owned subsidiaries located on foreign soil. Instead of producing products or services, either domestically or abroad for overseas sales, firms contract the right to produce directly to foreigners. Firms obtain income directly by providing resources, technology, expertise, trade names, or business designs to foreign producers. The foreign enterprise then owns and operates the business activity. Thus, while the originating firm establishes a presence in the global marketplace, that presence is usually quite modest, involving neither ownership nor control of the foreign operation.

Licensing

One of the primary methods of participating in new markets through cooperative contractual means is by licensing the firm's products, services, or technology to another company. Under this arrangement, the firm sells a limited right to produce and market the product in return for royalty payments. The typical limit is a specified geographic area in which the original firm does not market, at least to any significant degree.

Licensing to foreign companies has always played a prominent role in business strategies in advanced capitalist economies. With Japanese companies alone, U.S. firms entered into approximately 32,000 licensing agreements between 1952 and 1980.[1] Moreover, the pace of international licensing arrangements is increasing. Currently, licensing fees and royalty payments are earning U.S. licensers in excess of $12 billion a year, roughly twice the rate earned a decade earlier.[2]

International licensing was pursued initially in agreements between large, dominant firms in different countries, such as the cross-licensing arrangements between Du Pont and Imperial Chemical before World War II. These agreements granted each company exclusive rights to the other's technology within its own market area, thus avoiding direct competition between the dominant firms on the two sides of the Atlantic.

Manufacturers of military aircraft and other weapon systems have licensed foreign manufacturers for many years. McDonnell Douglas's F-15 fighter aircraft has been produced in Japan by Mitsubishi Heavy Industries working with Kawasaki Heavy Industries. Japanese firms have also made, under license, the Lockheed P-3C, the Boeing Chinook helicopter, the Bell Huey and Cobra helicopters, as well as the Patriot, Hawk, Sparrow, Sidewinder, and TOW missiles. Lockheed's F-104 fighter was coproduced in Germany for NATO. Korean firms have manufactured, under license, Northrop's F-5 aircraft, the M-109 Howitzer, and the McDonnell Douglas 500 MD helicopter. Companies in Taiwan have produced Northrop's F-5s, Bell's Huey helicopter, and several missiles, all under license from the U.S. firms.[3]

The more recent growth of international licensing has been paced by smaller firms in industries protected by patents, such as biotechnology, semiconductor, and pharma-

ceutical companies, that often lack the experience or resources needed to enter global markets directly.[4] Smaller
companies enjoy less bureaucracy and are thus capable of
moving through R&D faster. Because of their small size,
however, they are often unable to produce and market on a
scale large enough to recover R&D costs. Licensing is a way
for such firms to increase their returns on R&D. For instance, Immunex Corp., a biotechnology firm based in
Seattle, Washington, was able to develop seven products
for less than $85 million. It licensed five of them to larger
companies such as Hoffmann–La Roche, Syntex Corp., and
Eastman Kodak Co.[5]

Licensing frequently takes the form of a cross-licensing
agreement or technology swap between firms. This occurs
when two or more firms decide to share complementary technologies or production techniques. Thus, in 1987, when Motorola wanted to return to the dynamic random access memory (DRAM) business it lost in the early 1980s, the company
licensed some of its proprietary microprocessor designs to
Toshiba in return for DRAM production technology.[6]

In addition, the licensing of technology may also be
part of a larger, overall strategic partnership between firms,
a common practice for many successful firms engaging in
R&D cooperatives or joint ventures. Conversely, licensing
arrangements might evolve into a joint venture or other
strategic alliance. For instance, a major North American
electronics company converted a long-standing licensing
agreement with a manufacturer in the Philippines into a
joint venture when the licensing arrangement was no longer
suitable for both firms.[7]

Advantages

The primary advantage of licensing is that it allows firms to
earn some profits on existing products or technologies without making any significant new investment, either in marketing or production. This approach is especially helpful to
smaller firms that lack the financial and managerial re-

sources for establishing a more ambitious presence overseas. Licensing generally produces lower revenues than manufacturing locally, however, even when firms can charge an optimal licensing fee.[8] Royalty rates seldom exceed 5 percent of sales, and agreements are usually limited to 5 to 10 years, often not sufficient to recover high product-development costs.[9]

In the case of some high-technology industries, such as aerospace, licensing results in more than a flow of royalties and fees. Most of the content of products produced abroad under U.S. license – notably components and avionics – comes from U.S. manufacturers, bolstering direct exports. U.S. content, however, usually declines over the life of the product.

In addition, licensing arrangements can be made with foreign firms in exchange for market entry when barriers exist. These obstacles may include local political or industrial pressures, local distribution systems strongly favoring home-produced products, import restrictions and tariff barriers, and heavy transportation costs.[10] The firm can thus respond to an attractive overseas market without directly penetrating it. Some U.S. workstation manufacturers have established licensing partnerships with Japanese firms desiring to enter the worldwide workstation market in return for access to the lucrative Japanese market.[11]

Disadvantages

A primary disadvantage of licensing is loss of control and accountability. Once a contract has been signed, the foreign operator controls the manufacturing, marketing, and distribution of the product, the only restrictions being specified in the agreement. "It's very hard to control what happens to your product," says James T. Conte, senior vice president at ASI Market Research–Japan.[12] This fear keeps many firms away from entering into cooperative contractual relationships.

Similarly, the licenser usually does not have authority to determine the volume of production or the marketing strategy used. Furthermore, the brand or company name may also suffer because of poor production quality by the licensee. The enforcement of licensing agreements is usually best accomplished by the promise of new generations of technology, product line extensions, or improvements in production techniques. The threat not to renew the licensing arrangement then may be the most effective sanction available to the licenser.[13]

Some control issues can be resolved by negotiating strict quality or procedural guidelines into the contractual agreement. These agreements, however, typically require complex and detailed negotiations before contracts are actually signed, usually to ensure that the licensing firms are properly compensated. Once the agreement is signed, compliance is often difficult to monitor and enforce. This is especially true in countries in which patent laws and the legal system do not provide adequate protection for licensing contracts initiated by foreign companies.

Another critical disadvantage of licensing is that the technology a firm licenses to a foreign company may result in future competition from the licensee, a problem that can be severe after the expiration of the license.[14] Strong patent protection, however, may reduce the danger of such competition.[15] Nevertheless, this competition is one of the primary complaints made by companies that enter into licensing arrangements with competitors or potential competitors. Several of the Japanese color television producers that successfully penetrated the U.S. market are former licensees of RCA. Yamaha's entry into the U.S. musical instruments market followed the expiration of patents held by leading U.S. companies.

Cultural and language barriers may make it difficult for firms to structure contracts that are favorable to their company's long-range strategies. For example, the contracts may differ depending on whether the firm is affiliated with a West German company or an enterprise in India. In West Germany, assertiveness and achievement are highly valued, as they are in the United States. Thus, a U.S. company may be able to negotiate favorable contracts in much the same way two firms would transact business in the United States. India, however, has a traditional and well-structured social system that favors social relationships over money and achievement. Such a cultural system resists technologies that could disturb the power structure. Consequently, a foreign firm negotiating a licensing agreement in India may be required to make the contract more favorable for India as a way of lowering the social or cultural barrier to the entry of foreign technologies into the country.[16]

As Union Carbide found out, however, even though India may insist that local interests must dominate the partnership and determine the technology and manpower used, the large foreign firm is assigned the responsibility if things go badly wrong.

The Decision to License

U.S. businesses that successfully enter into licensing arrangements with foreign companies usually have to consider many aspects of the technology transfer, including the economic, political, and social implications at home and in the host country.

Reasons to License.   Licensing is beneficial when firms seek to learn more about a foreign market, such as the one in which the licensee operates. The knowledge and understanding gathered can then be used to determine whether a significant enough market exists to justify a more extensive capital investment. For instance, a small or mid-size company can penetrate a competitive foreign market by licensing a portion of its operations or technology to an overseas licensee for a short period. If the licensed product performs well, the company may then decide to enter the market directly by either exporting or setting up production facilities locally.[17]

Companies that desire to protect patents or other intangible assets may consider international licensing arrangements useful.[18] This approach may be necessary when patent infringement by foreign firms results in increased competition with U.S. businesses. Licensing is thus preferred in technologies that are not complex and are mature and have strong, well-enforced patents.[19] When the U.S. International Trade Commission ruled in 1987 that Japanese chip makers had infringed on the original DRAM patents held by Texas Instruments, the Dallas-based company forced foreign firms to sign licensing contracts. These contracts, along with other long-term licensing agreements signed with companies such as Toshiba, Oki Semiconductor, Mitsubishi Electric, Hitachi, and Samsung Electronics, have resulted in royalty payments exceeding $300 million a year for Texas Instruments.[20]

Licensing is appropriate when a firm wants to establish compatible industrial standards across countries. For instance, a manufacturer of proprietary computer technology may license its designs to foreign manufacturers in an effort to increase the share of computer operators worldwide using its machines. In this way the company may be able to introduce future computer systems more readily, not only because the company will have already established a prominent presence overseas, but also because the foreign enterprise will have incorporated the firm's computer systems within its operations. This approach was adopted by Eastman Kodak, which developed a method for storing color photographs on compact disks. To establish the new technology as a standard for still imaging, Kodak openly licensed the system to companies that wanted to utilize the manufacturing process.[21]

Consequently, new products by the same company will be more easily adapted into the activities of the foreign purchaser than disparate systems introduced by competitors. This may be particularly important as rapid technological advances make existing computers obsolete at a faster rate. Some countries, however, may resist adopting common standards originating in other nations, believing that such action would undermine national sovereignty or pride.[22]

Companies that have difficulty introducing products in the United States because of delayed approval or stricter governmental requirements can license their products to firms in other countries to introduce them to markets more quickly.[23] On other occasions, licensing is appropriate in the case of technologies associated with products that are no longer produced or that possess potential in an area not of strategic interest to the company.[24]

Reasons Not to License. Licensing arrangements are not favorable when the firm believes that the profit opportunities will be greater from opening up or expanding direct operations overseas than from simply licensing production to foreign companies. Similarly, licensing may not be attractive when the firm has domestic excess capacity and thus wishes to explore export markets more fully. This approach, however, requires the firm to overcome overseas barriers to trade. Similarly, licensing is generally not preferable with technologies that are firm-specific or that exhibit a large minimum efficient scale relative to total world output. In these cases, direct foreign investment may be more favorable.[25]

Licensing is also not beneficial when strong links exist between research and marketing, such as in the automobile and telecommunication industries.[26] Products that require extensive market research as a part of development may not generate substantial revenues when simply licensed in other markets. In these instances, firms would be likely to profit from a joint venture or other strategic alliance with the prospective licensee, so that product development and marketing can incorporate local market features.

Finally, a firm may decide to pursue strategies other than licensing when it does not wish to relinquish control of the product's marketing and distribution or when it fears potential competition from the partner as a result of the agreement. In 1988, for example, the United States and

Japan signed an agreement to produce an advanced support fighter for Japan's defense forces, the FSX. The arrangement was based on transferring the airframe technology of the U.S. F–16 from General Dynamics through license to Mitsubishi Heavy Industries. The agreement goes beyond earlier aircraft coproduction arrangements with Japan, however, and includes joint development of new technology.

This controversial project is a compromise – Japan neither does the entire project on its own nor does it rely entirely on U.S. know-how. Neither side is totally pleased. Many Americans fear that the work on the F–16/FSX will enable Japan to develop an independent, competing aerospace industry early in the twenty-first century. They would prefer outright sales of the U.S. product. In contrast, many Japanese resent the pressure to "share" their market with a U.S. firm.

Another cross-border project is the licensed production by the South Korean manufacturer Samsung of F–16 fighters. Unlike the arrangement with Japan, this agreement involves no codevelopment. South Korea will buy U.S. manufactured engines to power the aircraft. Samsung will eventually manufacture many of the parts, but not those incorporating the most critical technology.[27]

Franchising

Franchising is a variation of the licensing method in which the franchiser licenses an entire business system or service to an independent franchisee. In the United States, the franchise is becoming the fastest growing method of doing business.[28] Currently, one out of every three dollars Americans spend in retail establishments is claimed by franchised businesses. Many analysts expect a continuation of this trend, resulting perhaps in one out of every two consumer dollars being spent at franchised outlets sometime in the next century.[29]

While the franchise business booms in the most developed nations in the West, franchisers are realizing the enormous potential for business in overseas markets in less developed nations. At present, more than 400 U.S. franchising companies operate roughly 40,000 outlets internationally, triple the number in 1971. Consequently, traditional U.S. brand names such as Coca Cola, 7-Eleven, Mrs. Field's, Kentucky Fried Chicken, Pearle, Century 21, Dairy Queen, Tiffany's, and McDonald's are common in dozens of countries. As an illustration of the current pace of global franchising, McDonald's is believed to be opening a new international outlet at the rate of one every 18 minutes.

Some analysts attribute the increase in international franchising to a convergence of consumer preferences worldwide.[30] This convergence is neither uniform nor complete, because many differences in consumer desires for specific products and services remain. The demand for contemporary-style services in foreign lands is rising, however. This makes sophisticated marketing know-how and retailing experience valuable to overseas businesses and provides a larger market for franchising firms.[31]

In addition, many well-established companies are being approached by foreigners interested in purchasing the franchising rights for their country or territory. Popeye's Famous Fried Chicken successfully entered markets in Singapore and Malaysia when local food-service operators expressed an interest in acquiring the Popeye's license.[32] Being approached initially is an ideal means of introducing franchising abroad, but only when prospective buyers are able to show that local markets exist for the products or services provided by the franchise and that they have the requisite capital and management capability.

The franchising method of operating in the global marketplace is most prominent in the service industries, especially in fast food. In Taiwan, U.S. fast food franchises are located alongside traditional street vendors selling snake blood and turtle soup.[33] McDonald's became one of the first U.S. firms to penetrate the Russian economy when it opened a restaurant in Moscow in January 1990. This outlet, located near the Kremlin, is the largest McDonald's anywhere. It serves between 40,000 and 50,000 people a day. Pizza Hut and Baskin-Robbins are also located in Moscow.

Other food outlets that have succeeded internationally include Kentucky Fried Chicken, one of the first to go abroad and now one of the most successful chains in Japan. Domino's Pizza, Arby's, Dairy Queen, Wendy's, and Subway Sandwiches are flourishing in Asia. Dunkin' Donuts is very popular in the Middle East.

Additional business sectors using the franchising approach to respond to the globalization of the world economy include business aids and services, auto services, construction and maintenance businesses, and retail and convenience stores. Fantastic Sam's, a popular hair-salon chain, sold its franchise rights in Japan in 1988. Jiffy Lube, Hertz, Budget Rent-A-Car, and Dollar Rent-A-Car are well established in Europe and Asia. Other services, such as Rainbow International, a carpet dyeing and cleaning company based in Texas, and Mailboxes Etc., both strong businesses in the United States, have sold franchising rights in the United Kingdom.[34]

The most popular form of franchising worldwide, comprising a majority of all international franchises, is the master license right or master franchise. Under this format, the franchiser sells the license or territorial rights to an individual, business group, or corporation. The purchaser, or franchisee, then controls all operations within the territory. It may either operate outlets on its own or issue subfranchises within the territory. The master franchisee pays royalty fees to the licensing firm, usually between 1 and 10 percent of gross revenues.[35]

Another type of franchise is the joint venture, in which the U.S. firm teams up with a local individual, company or government group within the targeted territory.[36] This is the form used by McDonald's in Moscow, which established a joint relationship with the City Council.

Advantages

As with licensing, franchising offers companies quick access to foreign markets without the need for large foreign investments. Moreover, by selling the master franchise rights to a country, the gain in market exposure increases the recognition of the franchised company's name, an added benefit in today's highly competitive international marketplace.

Another benefit of franchising, particularly master franchising, is the "upfront money" a firm receives when it sells the franchising rights to a large geographical area.[37] Even with the joint venture franchise, which usually requires an investment by both partners, royalty payments and other fees are a significant source of additional operating funds.

Franchising also allows firms to use proven marketing strategies to target a specific market segment. Mr. Build Handi-Man Services, a company that recently negotiated the master franchising rights in the United Kingdom, targets two-income families who do not want to spend their free time doing home improvements.[38]

Disadvantages

International franchising is not well suited for all business activities because it is primarily geared to service and consumer-oriented businesses. Franchising does not operate well in high-technology industries or in manufacturing generally.

Another disadvantage with franchising abroad is similar to licensing – the loss of control once the franchising agreement is signed. Although contracts can incorporate quality and consistency requirements, firms have difficulty overseeing all aspects of the franchising operation.[39] This is particularly true in developing countries where heavy-handed governmental intervention and political instability make monitoring local operations difficult.

Cultural or language barriers may also inhibit the effectiveness of franchising abroad. Franchising is predominantly a U.S. marketing strategy and thus may not be suited to all cultures. As the globalization of economies continues, however, and as businesses learn to become more responsive to local needs and preferences, franchising may be an effective means of targeting different segments within a host country.

The Decision to Franchise

The decision to franchise abroad is an important element of a firm's overall strategic response to world competition. Before establishing foreign franchise operations, a firm will consider several factors.

Reasons to Franchise. In a study conducted by the International Franchise Association in 1988, franchisers stated that of those that have been successful most consider only countries that are politically stable and have a substantial middle class with disposable income.[40] An illustration of the difficulties of local political instability is Pizza Hut's experience in Moscow, where one of its two restaurants closed temporarily for alleged health violations. In reality, the shutdown was the result of a political power struggle between the Moscow City Council and the District Council.[41]

The regulatory climate of potential host countries is also a factor in determining whether to expand outside the home country. Developing nations often discriminate against franchising by foreign firms because this type of business arrangement is seen as merely a "marketing" system rather than a contribution to economic growth. Effective franchisers are also concerned with such issues as child labor laws and the need to specify products in the metric system.[42]

Even within a single geographic area, countries may differ significantly in the degree to which they allow franchising. In East Asia, South Korea generally discourages franchising, unless joint ventures are established giving the local franchisee 50 percent or more ownership. Taiwan, Thailand, Indonesia, and the Philippines usually allow franchising as joint ventures, while Hong Kong has no restrictions on franchising arrangements.[43] Before seeking potential international franchising partners, many firms try to understand more fully the country in which they wish to locate, including the socioeconomic conditions as well as any potential governmental restraints on their activities, particularly eligibility requirements such as having a local equity partner.

Reasons Not to Franchise.   All experts agree that franchising overseas is never appropriate if the parent firm is not well established domestically. Successful international franchisers take their domestic strengths and weaknesses with them when they locate in other nations.[44] Companies are advised to solidify their domestic positions before deciding on growing internationally.

Franchising abroad is especially risky when it is difficult to sustain supply channels for the franchise outlet and when variations in quality, consistency, and costs are great. In Moscow, McDonald's has experienced considerable trouble finding suitable sources of raw materials, and Pepsi worries about the varying quality of its product, which is dispensed in paper cups or cracked glasses in drink stands around the city.[45]

Finally, franchisers seeking to expand to foreign lands need to be aware of the pressure to alter the product or service to fit local tastes or customs. To be willing to do so often requires extensive understanding of the foreign market, society, and culture. Kentucky Fried Chicken had difficulty with its first three stores in Japan during the 1960s because of its strict adherence to the original formula for its chicken batter. Today, however, it has become enormously successful by using chickens raised in Japan, which satisfy local size and quality requirements, as well as by taking scrupulous care of its cooking oil, customer service, and shop sanitation.[46]

Moreover, McDonald's in Japan changed the name of its mascot Ronald McDonald to Donald McDonald and the pronunciation of its own name to "Makudonaldo," both of which are easier for the Japanese to pronounce. Pizza Time Theatre was required to make major modifications in its menu in Malaysia and the Middle East because pork and dairy items are unacceptable to the local customers.[47]

Subcontracting

Another method of engaging in cooperative contractual business relationships with foreign firms is through subcontracting. Also known as outsourcing, subcontracting refers to an agreement in which one company contracts to another a specific production task or segment of its business operation. These contracts may be long-standing, as part of a buyer-supplier relationship, or they may be temporary agreements that end when the contracted activity is completed.

Subcontracting also encompasses agreements ranging from the purchase of foreign-made components that are assembled in the home country of the enterprise to the complete production of products by manufacturers overseas. Contracts securing the production of goods by foreign manufacturers are to be distinguished from foreign direct investments, in which the parent company builds and operates its own production facilities overseas.[48]

Subcontracting has traditionally been important in the construction and aerospace industries, where the complexity of production necessarily involves the contracting of particular operations to specialized firms. Furthermore, international outsourcing is also a significant part of the automobile industry's operations. For instance, Ford Motor Company receives axles for its passenger cars and manual transmissions for its smaller trucks from Mazda. Ford also has agreements with Yamaha in Japan, Cosworth in the

United Kingdom, and Porsche in Germany for the design and development of some of the car engines used in the models it produces in Europe.[49]

Subcontracting is becoming increasingly essential in other industries as global competition forces firms to shorten product development times and reduce costs. This is because the development and production of products rely heavily on so many different technologies that no single firm can sustain a competitive advantage in all of them.[50] Consequently, many firms are responding by farming out work to those foreign or domestic companies that are able to produce quality products most efficiently or at the lowest cost.

Subcontracting is also growing because of technological developments that have facilitated the ability of firms in a great variety of countries to process information and maintain rigid quality standards. These advances in technology, along with a proliferation of sources worldwide, have made it increasingly possible for companies to search for and secure the services of foreign operators possessing cost, technical, or locational advantages.[51]

More and more multinational firms are thus becoming the designers or architects of products produced in large measure by specialized subcontractors located in different parts of the world. Traditionally, commercial aircraft manufacturers have contracted the design and production of engines to other firms, such as the UK's Rolls-Royce or the United States' General Electric and Pratt and Whitney (the latter a division of United Technologies). More recently, large computer companies, such as International Business Machines Corp. (IBM), have begun teaming up with smaller firms to secure their unique market niches. The smaller firms benefit from the credibility associated with working alongside a giant computer company. In turn, they allow IBM to occupy markets it would otherwise have been unable to exploit, while ensuring that the niche products are tailored for IBM machines. Says a former IBM executive,

"IBM is turning itself into an architect and general contractor, rather than a piece-parts supplier," a trend being followed by other major global companies.[52]

Subcontracting refers not only to a contractual agreement in which a firm farms out an activity: the company can also profit from international sourcing relationships by being a subcontractor to another enterprise. For example, General Motors contracts with Isuzu to supply transmissions and other parts for the U.S. company and also sells components to eight Japanese firms. In 1989, its sales in this capacity totaled $135 million.[53]

As with licensing and franchising agreements, contracts for outsourcing are often part of a variety of strategic interfirm relationships. For instance, a large manufacturing firm may establish cooperative, longer-term partnerships with its key suppliers. The costs of coordination, however, may make it uneconomical to do so with a host of smaller suppliers. In the latter case, a focus on short-term arrangements and cost competition may well be the most effective approach.

Furthermore, many suppliers actively participate in the design and development of the products requested by contracting firms. More than half of U.S. suppliers take part in all or most of the design of the contractor's products, if necessary filling in details. In many other cases, the firms share the design work. Only 5 percent of U.S. suppliers report that the contractor takes the entire responsibility.[54]

Advantages

Subcontracting represents an ideal strategy if a firm wishes to specialize in the design or production of core components or technologies by leaving peripheral production to other companies.[55] Sun Microsystems, Inc., a maker of workstations for engineers and technicians, became one of the fastest growing companies in its industry by contracting with such Japanese companies as Toshiba and Tokyo Electron Laboratories to manufacture finished computers. This arrangement allowed

Sun to focus on its proprietary design, software, and marketing expertise.[56] This approach, however, necessitates a commitment on the part of the company to work closely with its sourcing partners, especially when the exchange of proprietary information is involved and when products rely heavily on rapidly changing technologies.

One of the principal advantages of subcontracting is cost reduction. Foreign suppliers often offer less expensive and less restrictive work rules, as well as lower land and facility costs, than domestic or in-house sources. Lower costs are the primary motive for approximately one-third to one-half of the U.S. companies currently seeking international subcontracting arrangements.[57]

In the apparel industry, New York–based Gitano has its products made in many underdeveloped countries. Gitano trains the workers, provides the equipment, and often contributes to the development of the necessary infrastructure. Then, when labor wages begin to rise as other manufacturers enter the area, Gitano looks elsewhere for lower labor costs. On the other hand, a firm that maintains its product sources in the developing country even when labor wages rise can expect increased sales of its own products in the country as it becomes wealthier.[58]

Other advantages of global subcontracting are the substantial benefits industrial contractors and suppliers can gain from knowing each other's products and processes. Globally oriented companies can acquire a sustainable competitive advantage by securing access to innovative technologies overseas, thus locking competitors out of the technological base. In the case of the automobile industry, the proportion of U.S. companies that provide their statistical process control charts to firms they supply with parts rose from 16 percent in 1984 to 92 percent in 1989.[59]

Disadvantages

A fundamental disadvantage with subcontracting is the potential loss in flexibility and control that results when a firm eliminates its own production capacity through a contract with another firm. By contracting the manufacturing of highly technological components or products to foreign producers, firms risk not only their R&D capabilities but also their ability to manufacture more advanced products cost efficiently in the future.[60] The slow start by U.S. companies in the development of high-definition television (HDTV) is the consequence of outsourcing agreements for Japanese-made video cassette recorders (VCRs). These contracts reduced the extent to which U.S. firms could efficiently manufacture succeeding generations of the VCR, which was the forerunner of HDTV technology.[61]

Similarly, outsourcing may result in a deepening dependence on foreign partners as a source of key components, as well as a source of future product development and design capabilities.[62] This has been the complaint of makers of flat-panel displays, semiconductor equipment, specialized computer chips, and machine tools, who rely on foreign manufacturers for key components. They have repeatedly accused Japanese companies of selectively withholding parts in an effort to gain a competitive advantage.[63]

Yet another disadvantage of international subcontracting is the adverse sentiment a firm may generate domestically when jobs are lost as production or other business activities are shifted to foreign sources.

At times the expense of negotiating, maintaining, and enforcing contracts outweighs the gains from use of lower-cost alternative production sites. Moreover, other expenses associated with obtaining supplies from outside the company may make outsourcing an undesirable strategy. For instance, obtaining products, or sourcing, from a partner in Asia may add 10 to 15 percent to the unit costs when transportation and other distribution charges are considered. Because of lag times of as much as six or eight weeks, inventory buffers are required, further increasing the direct costs of subcontracting with foreign companies. Finally, if foreign-made products require extensive design changes or some other reworking of the product resulting in substantially higher unit costs, firms may decide to look elsewhere or maintain production in-house.[64]

Conclusion

As in the other responses to the global marketplace, firms entering into cooperative contractual agreements show no single pattern for success. To be sure, successes abound in the use of overseas licensing, franchising, and subcontracting, particularly as a way of getting around import restrictions or investment barriers established by foreign governments. Nevertheless, the failures and marginal results, which do not receive as much public attention, are equally important lessons from the globalization of business.

4

Building and Buying
Overseas Operations

A well-established and still popular method for securing a business presence abroad is for a company to buy or
build production and distribution facilities in a foreign
country. Indeed, despite the attention to strategic alliances
in the popular literature, most overseas operations of U.S.
manufacturing multinationals in developing countries are
wholly owned.[1] So are the divisions of most U.S. companies
operating in Europe.[2] Of the high-growth companies be-
longing to the American Business Conference, fully one-
third entered foreign markets through either the construction of new facilities or the acquisition of existing ones.[3]

The primary exception occurs when the host country
places restrictions on the extent of ownership by foreign
businesses. These may be formal investment barriers, less
formal but often equally powerful barriers in the form of tax
breaks to competing local companies, and local content
laws requiring local producers to use locally made supplies.[4]
For these reasons, in Asia and in Eastern Europe joint ventures and other strategic alliances are the dominant modes
used by foreign companies attempting to develop a presence in local markets (see chapters 5 and 6).

In some circumstances, a host government may be willing to accept the construction, expansion, or acquisition of a local branch by a U.S. company on the condition that the firm meets a specified performance requirement or other concession. Before IBM was allowed to expand its operations in Mexico, the company agreed to set up a development center for semiconductors, purchase high-technology components from Mexican companies, and produce software for Latin America in Mexico.[5]

IBM is often cited as the role model for foreign firms focusing on high-technology markets. Potential imitators note that the corporation's basic research laboratories are in Switzerland and Japan, as well as the United States. Its 30-odd research divisions are located around the world. The process of international technology transfer at IBM is thus often internal to the firm – a firm that surely represents the progression to the borderless laboratory.

Pharmaceutical firms are not too far behind. Merck & Co. has laboratories in Canada, the United Kingdom, France, Spain, Italy, and Japan. Xerox Corporation is another interesting example of global operations. Xerox has introduced some 80 different office copying machines in the United States that were engineered and built by its Japanese joint venture, Fuji Xerox Company.

United Technologies exemplifies the use of geographic diversification on a global scale in developing new products. The company operates more than 120 manufacturing plants in 24 countries. With sales and service offices in more than 56 countries, it is represented in virtually every country of the world. Its new elevator, the Elevonic 411, presents a cogent case in point. The French branch of the Otis Elevator division of United Technologies worked on the door systems; the Spanish division handled the small-geared components; the German subsidiary was responsible for the electronics; the Japanese unit designed the special motor drives; and the Connecticut group handled the systems integration. International teamwork cut the development cycle in half.[6]

Advantages

Owning and operating foreign production facilities gives the firm maximum freedom, control over initiatives, and all of the profit resulting from its efforts. Thus, for most companies operating abroad, the establishment of a wholly owned subsidiary is their first choice compared to other strategies, such as licensing or forming joint ventures.

Producing overseas is also an effective way for a company to overcome import restrictions. Market penetration is likely to be greater than under exporting, and profit potentials are larger than with licensing (and sales are not limited to the host country). The costs of R&D are spread over more units, as are the centralized expenses. The parent company, in the process of producing and then selling overseas, learns about foreign markets and ways of doing business overseas.[7]

Operating abroad allows firms the option of selecting the most favorable production locations in terms of infrastructure maintenance, tax treatment, and local government regulation. This is particularly true in contestable markets or where capital is highly mobile. Political pressures at home, however, may make this option difficult to follow. Yet the fact that an increasing number of firms are devoting resources to their design and production facilities abroad suggests that governments are experiencing a reduction in their ability to restrict business activity. Moreover, permanent increases in business taxes as part of a sustained anti-inflationary effort in the home country, for example, may encourage businesses to shift production overseas.[8]

Disadvantages

The use of wholly owned production affiliates abroad is not without its difficulties. Most notable is the large investment required when firms build plants overseas or acquire another company. Operating wholly owned subsidiaries outside the United States may be politically difficult, at home as well as in the host nation—especially if the motivation to produce abroad is to capitalize on cheaper labor costs and then ship the products back to the United States.

In some industries, the search for lower labor costs is not the primary motivation for moving production facilities outside the United States. In the production of sophisticated capital goods, for instance, labor is a declining part of total product costs.[9] In these industries, a favorable regulatory climate and the opportunity to obtain components of high quality at low prices may influence a firm's decision to produce abroad.

Acquiring a foreign business with the intent of operating it as a wholly owned subsidiary may also produce strong negative reactions locally. In many business circles in Japan, for example, mergers and acquisitions are still considered to be antisocial activities.[10] In such instances, a joint venture, licensing, or other cooperative alliance may be a more viable means of operating within the local market.

It is interesting to note the public justification given by the president of Japan's Banyu Pharmaceutical Corporation on the occasion of a friendly takeover by Merck:

> Since Banyu and Merck have trusted each other through friendly business relations which have lasted for over 30 years, we have no concern whatsoever about giving Merck controlling interest in Banyu. . . . Banyu will continue with the Japanese style personnel administration and labor management practices as before . . . paying due respect to the traditions of and business customs and practices prevailing in the Japanese pharmaceutical industry.[11]

Direct Foreign Investment

A primary method of developing a foreign business presence is through greenfield operations—building a new manufacturing plant or establishing a new division in another country. Overseas investment has traditionally been important in industries in which proximity to the local market has been important, such as perishable food products. In contrast, that concern is negligible in industries such as aerospace, which is characterized by high fixed costs, scale economies, and ease of transporting the end product.[12] Steel is an example of an intermediate case in which low value-to-weight structural components are usually made closer to the customer, while higher value-to-weight specialty products may be shipped over long distances.

Worldwide outflows of foreign direct investment have increased nearly 29 percent a year on average since 1983, three times the growth rate of world exports. In 1989, the total stock of foreign investment worldwide was approximately $1.5 trillion, four-fifths of which came from the United States, the EC, and Japan.[13]

Moreover, U.S. companies have been investing at a more rapid rate in overseas affiliates than in their domestic divisions. From 1987 to 1990, domestic capital spending by U.S. businesses grew on average at 9 percent a year compared with a 21 percent increase overseas.[14]

About one-half of current overseas investment by U.S. firms is going into the European Community, with the largest share going to locations in the United Kingdom. Other significant capital investments by U.S. firms are being made in Canada, Latin America, and the Pacific Rim area (see table 4.1).

As has been true for a long time, the petroleum industry continues to make the largest U.S. investments overseas, three times that of the second-place chemical industry (see table 4.2). The current rapid expansion of burdensome regulations in the United States is likely to accelerate the tendency of U.S. firms to expand overseas.[15]

Foreign investment by transnational companies has been facilitated by a number of important factors, including a global convergence of technologies, consumer tastes, and national policies, as in the EC. In addition, a proliferation of production locations worldwide has provided alternative and competitive sites for companies that wish to expand

TABLE 4.1
Capital Outlays by Foreign Affiliates of U.S. Companies,
by Area, Calendar Years 1987–1991
(billions of U.S. dollars)

Location	1987	1988	1989	1990	1991[a]
Canada	6.5	7.9	8.9	9.6	8.4
European Community	16.1	19.8	24.0	31.2	32.2
Other Europe	1.6	1.8	2.1	2.5	2.7
Japan	1.2	1.8	2.0	2.1	2.2
Australia & New Zealand	1.9	2.6	3.4	2.6	2.8
Subtotal, developed nations	27.3	33.9	40.4	47.9	48.4
Latin America	3.3	3.6	4.6	5.1	5.6
Africa	0.7	0.9	0.9	1.4	1.5
Middle East	0.5	0.4	0.5	0.8	0.8
Other Asia	2.2	3.0	4.1	5.1	5.8
Subtotal, developing nations	6.7	8.0	10.2	12.4	13.6
Multinational affiliates	0.4	0.7	0.9	1.0	1.1
Total	34.4	42.6	51.5	61.2	63.1

Source: Survey of Current Business, March 1992, p. 44.
[a]Estimated.

operations abroad. This is particularly true as a result of the opening of Eastern Europe to foreign investment.[16]

Innovations in world capital markets have also facilitated increases in foreign direct investment in developing nations. By purchasing a portion of a country's external debt at a discount through the open market and then selling the debt to the host country's central bank, a foreign firm can receive local currency to make investments. The use of such debt-equity swaps is common in South Ameri-

TABLE 4.2
Capital Outlays by Foreign Affiliates of U.S. Companies,
by Industry, Calendar Years 1987–1991
(billions of U.S. dollars)

Industry	1987	1988	1989	1990	1991[a]
Petroleum	9.8	13.3	13.2	16.7	19.7
Chemicals	3.7	4.7	5.5	6.8	6.5
Transportation equipment	3.4	3.6	4.6	6.0	5.8
Machinery	3.0	3.4	4.1	4.7	4.3
Electric/electronic equipment	1.7	2.1	2.3	2.6	2.7
Other manufacturing	5.4	6.6	8.9	9.3	8.9
Subtotal, manufacturing	17.2	20.4	25.3	29.4	28.2
Wholesale trade	2.6	3.2	3.9	4.4	4.5
Finance, insurance, and real estate	1.0	0.8	1.6	2.1	1.7
Services	1.7	2.1	3.4	3.6	3.3
All other	2.1	2.8	4.0	5.1	5.8
Total	34.4	42.6	51.5	61.3	63.1

Source: Survey of Current Business, March 1992, p. 44.
[a]Estimated.

ca. For instance, 80 percent of all foreign direct investment in Chile currently utilizes the debt-equity method of entry. In Brazil, Mexico, and Argentina, the percentage of total investment through debt-equity swaps is 59, 30, and 20 percent respectively.[17]

The Decision to Invest Overseas

Of the considerations facing a company seeking to expand its development or production operations into foreign markets, the choice of ownership structure is perhaps one of the most serious decisions to make. Typically, the desire for full ownership and the bargaining power relative to that of the host government play an important role.[18]

Reasons to Invest Abroad. The establishment of a new affiliate abroad normally occurs when the host government allows full ownership and the company is familiar with the local markets, customs, laws, and other idiosyncrasies associated with operating in another country.[19] Firms with internationally recognized brand names and globally recognized corporate names and quality reputations prefer to obtain the benefits of global advertising directly.

Reasons Not to Invest Abroad. The construction of overseas production facilities is often not feasible when the host government's policies prevent 100 percent ownership or when such ownership generates adverse political pressures. Even when governmental policies do not place restrictions on the full ownership of firms by foreigners, companies often find it in their interest to seek a partner who knows the market and is familiar with local distribution networks.[20] The combination of having to monitor costs and the high political risks makes licensing or joint ventures more attractive than greenfield operations.

This may be especially true for smaller companies lacking experience operating abroad or not possessing sufficient resources to construct a wholly owned operation. Small-size firms may initially form a joint venture with a local partner with the intention of buying out the partner later in order to obtain full ownership.[21]

At times, the firm has to acknowledge the painful fact that its overseas investment has not worked out as expected and must be cut back. In March 1992, Federal Express announced such a retrenchment. It turned over local deliveries in many European countries to local firms and took a $254 million restructuring charge. Federal Express concluded that the strategy it had used to create the overnight delivery market in the United States did not work in Europe.[22]

Mergers and Acquisitions

Mergers and acquisitions are two related but distinctive forms of business combination. A merger unites two or more businesses into a single enterprise. An acquisition, on the other hand, is an instance of one company getting possession of another company; only the acquired firm loses its identity.[23] For tax and other technical reasons, the distinction between the two approaches may at times be blurred.

Acquisitions are playing an increasingly important role in the expansion of global firms into foreign markets. Indeed, the wave of takeovers and buyouts of businesses within the United States has obscured the fact that cross-border transactions grew at a faster rate. From 1985 to 1989, international mergers and acquisitions involving U.S. companies grew fourfold, while the U.S. domestic volume remained essentially static. In 1985, business mergers within the United States accounted for 85 percent of global merger activity. By 1990, U.S. domestic mergers accounted for less than half of the worldwide volume. Most of the U.S. companies operating in Europe do so through subsidiaries resulting from acquisitions.[24]

Mergers and acquisitions can overcome the constraints imposed if the parent company's work force has a limited range of capabilities. Companies from countries with relatively low-cost capital will value foreign earning streams that are higher than financial markets within their own countries. Managerial risks, however, may be greater than in the case in which the global firm creates a new overseas subsidiary.

In general, firms acquire medium-size rather than large enterprises in attempting to penetrate foreign markets via acquisitions and mergers. As shown in table 4.3, only two U.S. mergers in 1990 involved European firms valued in excess of $500 million—Philip Morris bought Suchard of Switzerland and Ford acquired the UK's Jaguar. Other acquisitions ranged from $460 million (Emerson Electric taking over Leroy-Somer of France) to $25 million (SunTrust

Banks buying out the Graham Miller Group in the United Kingdom).

The process of acquiring or merging with another company is often difficult and lengthy. Merck's acquisition of a controlling interest in Japan's Banyu Pharmaceutical Corporation a decade ago was the first to involve a company from the prestigious first (or "blue chip") section of the Tokyo Stock Exchange.[25] A study of 180 U.S.-based multinationals in the 1970s revealed that 35 percent of the acquired local subsidiaries were subsequently liquidated or sold. The "mortality" rate of newly formed ventures averaged 22 percent.[26]

The Decision to Seek Mergers and Acquisitions

Mergers and acquisitions facilitate market entry and provide access to new technologies and talented people. On some occasions, they may yield an infusion of capital.[27]

Reasons to Merge with or Acquire a Foreign Firm. A merger or acquisition is often seen as potentially effective when the parent company and the acquired firm are closely related. A merger or acquisition may also be appropriate when the purchasing company's long-range goals require full control of the acquired firm or when the capabilities of an existing local enterprise are needed.[28] Objectives that are seen as short term or broadly structured may be served better by a nonequity strategic alliance or a simple licensing agreement.

Acquisitions are favorable when the costs of a joint venture are especially high and when the benefits of cooperation are sufficiently strong. The increase in the size of the firm, however, may lead to diseconomies of scale or additional costs associated with overseeing a larger organization.

Moreover, an acquisition may also result in a form of joint venture, such as when a company only purchases a part of the local firm's equity. Solving the problem of what degree of ownership to take often depends on the expected contributions of the local firm or whether necessary con-

TABLE 4.3
Top 20 U.S. Acquisitions of European Companies, 1990

Acquiring Company	Target Company	Target Country	Price (U.S. $millions)
1. Philip Morris Cos. Inc.	Jacobs Suchard Ltd.	Switzerland	$3,800
2. Ford Motor Co.	Jaguar PLC	UK	2,644
3. Emerson Electric Co.	Leroy-Somer	France	460
4. Goldman, Sachs & Co.	Wolters Kluwer NV	Netherlands	444
5. General Electric Co.	Burton Group Financial Services	UK	329
6. American Brands Inc.	Whyte & Mackay Distillers Ltd.	Scotland	274
7. CPC International Inc.	Three food businesses of SmithKline Beecham PLC	UK	255
8. International Paper Co.	Cookson Graphic Arts	UK	215
9. Old Bond Street Corp.	Yardley/Lentheric Cosmetics unit of SmithKline Beecham	UK	182
10. General Electric Co.	Tungsram Co. Ltd.	Hungary	150
11. Scott Paper Co.	Sanitary tissue business of Feldmuehle AG	Germany	130

12. Investco (a Morgan Stanley affiliate, and Fitzwilton PLC)	Waterford Wedgwood PLC	Ireland	112
13. John Head & Partners	Anglo American Insurance Co. Ltd.	UK	110
14. Philip Morris Cos. Inc.	Pietro Negroni SpA	Italy	81
15. Bristol-Myers Squibb	UPSA Group	France	80
16. IVAX Corp.	Harris-Pharmaceuticals Ltd.	UK	73
17. Allied-Signal Inc.	Brake-linings unit of Valeo SA	France	72
18. UNUM Corp.	National Employers Life Assurance Holding Co. Ltd.	UK	71
19. E. I. Du Pont de Nemours	UK North Sea interests of Triton Europe PLC	UK	61
20. Corporate Partners LP	Albert Fisher Group PLC	UK	52

Source: Directors and Boards, Spring 1991, p. 59.

tacts with other local business groups can only be maintained through the targeted company. Similarly, the difficulty of supervising foreign management may also play a role in the decision to acquire a local firm.[29]

Reasons for Not Merging with or Acquiring a Foreign Firm.   Some mergers and acquisitions turn out to be less effective than anticipated, especially when the value of an acquired firm is in the people. Executives and other key personnel typically leave soon after a change in control.[30]

A merger or acquisition also generates potential problems when the acquired firm is culturally different from the acquiring business. If it is anticipated that the acquired unit will remain dependent on the original parent company or owner, then it may be better to enter into some form of alliance. Outright acquisitions of foreign companies may not be particularly effective within industries that are highly regulated, such as financial services. In these cases, local governments may seek through prohibitive regulations concerning takeovers to ensure that control remains local.[31] Purchases of a minority stake may, however, be an attainable alternative.

Conclusion

Although attractive as a strategic response to global competition, the use of wholly owned affiliates, either through construction or acquisition, brings substantial contingent liability. This approach usually includes a substantial investment and ties the parent company to a long-term commitment to doing business in that market.

Nevertheless, firms that successfully compete on an international scale, especially the larger enterprises, include direct investment and the operation of wholly owned subsidiaries as key operations in their global strategy — when the host government allows such operations.

5

Strategic Alliances without Equity Investment

Strategic alliances across national borders have become the rage in some business circles. A primary reason for such partnerships is to create synergies not present when each of the partners acts alone. Strategic alliances are cooperative, flexible arrangements, born out of the mutual needs of firms to share the risks of an often uncertain marketplace by jointly pursuing a common objective.[1]

Strategic alliances are typically characterized in one of two different ways. The first, called a vertical, complementary, or x-type, involves agreements to cooperate in complementary activities. For instance, one firm may concentrate on the design and development of the product, while the other manufactures it.

The other type of strategic alliance, often referred to as a horizontal, joint, or y-type, involves cooperation within the same activity, such as a joint R&D venture or joint production agreement.[2] Horizontal agreements are common in the aerospace industry, in which firms are anxious to share the high cost and great risk involved in developing a new generation of jet airliners.

Strategic partnerships can take several different forms, depending on the specific nature of the objectives of the participating businesses.[3] For instance, firms may cooperate with other domestic companies to increase market share or to protect market share from foreign (or other domestic) competitors. Alliances may be formed with domestic companies for essentially domestic reasons, but the association may extend to international markets.

In the alliance that IBM and Apple entered into in October 1991, the two firms share their advanced technology but continue separate manufacturing operations. They also remain competitors in marketing their products. By working together — in effect, pooling their scientific talent — the two computer leaders hope to accomplish what neither company could alone: to develop a new array of technology and software that will revolutionize computing and raise demand in their beleaguered industry.[4]

Each company brings special characteristics to the partnership. Apple fears that its inability to convert to the IBM-dominated mainframe world threatens its survival. In turn, IBM lacks Apple's crucial software technologies. The two companies already face competing alliances, notably the ACE consortium, including Microsoft, Compaq, and Digital Equipment, which is built around a chip designed by MIPS Computer Systems. Another alliance, SPARC International, consists of 240 companies promoting the chip designed by Sun Microsystems. In the words of IBM president Jack Kuehler, "There is simply no way in the future for one company to do it all."[5]

Some alliances consist of simple cross-border partnerships, in which the United States participates in the foreign market with a local firm. Texas Instruments entered into a joint effort with three well-known Japanese electronics firms — Fujitsu, Hitachi, and Sony — to develop semiconductors for high-definition television sets sold in Japan.[6] Other cross-border alliances involve more complicated partnerships, such as the partnership of Southwestern Bell with France Telecom and Grupo Carso, a Mexican mining and manufacturing company, to acquire a controlling interest in Telefonos de Mexico, the Mexican national telephone company.[7]

Other alliances are true global ventures, in which multinational corporations cooperate with other global firms at several levels of the organization and in multiple locations, usually with the objective of expanding operations on a worldwide level. Examples of these alliances abound; a few of the more prominent partnerships include Motorola and Toshiba, General Motors and Toyota, AT&T and NEC, and the Airbus Consortium in Western Europe. In 1991, AT&T joined forces with British Telecom, France Telecom, and Kokusai Denshin Denwa to provide large customers with a global communications network capability.[8]

Strategic partnerships are not a new phenomenon. In 1897, Thomas Edison, founder of General Electric, formed a cooperative venture with Corning Glass Works to produce his experimental incandescent light bulbs.[9] Toshiba was also involved in forming alliances as early as 1906.[10] What is new is the increased frequency of the creation of cooperative associations and the diversity of industry and of nationality of firms involved and of the types and varieties of alliances into which companies enter.[11]

The pace at which cooperative strategic alliances between firms occur is accelerating, particularly in high-tech, high-growth industries, such as computers, semiconductors, telecommunications, electronics, chemicals, and industrial equipment.[12] The trend is evident in the aerospace and automotive industries, in which every major company has formed alliances with foreign competitors in an effort to spread the costs and risks of developing new products, as well as to ensure access to overseas markets.[13]

In the computer industry especially, corporate alliances have become so common that it is extremely difficult to distinguish between competitors and collaborators. According to John Akers, chief executive officer of IBM, "We all learn how to drink coffee together at ten and beat each other's brains out at two."[14]

IBM's experience in Japan furnishes a good example of the rapid pace of the development of strategic alliances. In 1980, IBM Japan owned and controlled its principal assets and sold its products through its own sales force. By 1988,

IBM Japan had created 17 joint ventures, set up relationships with 9 leasing firms, sold products through 136 dealers, allowed 107 other companies to remarket its products, and had formed working arrangements with nearly 800 software service organizations.[15] IBM Japan also has links with Ricoh in the distribution and sales of low-end computers, with Nippon Steel in systems integration, with Fuji Bank in financial systems, with OMRON in computer-integrated manufacturing, and with NTT in value-added networks.[16]

Before its alliance with Apple, IBM turned to Microsoft and Intel. Microsoft, which supplies the operating system of the personal computer (PC), was a partner in IBM software development throughout the 1980s. Intel, which produces the PC's microchip, has also been a long-term IBM supplier. In addition, during the mid-1980s, IBM owned 20 percent of Intel.[17]

Despite the attractiveness of the concept of strategic alliances in a worldwide economy, available data do not support the notion that joint ventures and other forms of interfirm alliances are becoming the most common way in which companies cross national borders. Table 5.1 presents data on the number and types of investment options undertaken by U.S. manufacturing companies from 1988 to 1990. Clearly, acquisitions continue to be the dominant corporate instrument for establishing a continuing presence overseas, accounting for 354 out of 668 overseas manufacturing investment activities during that recent three-year period.

Strategic alliances are the dominant mechanism used to participate in those national markets not fully open to foreign firms. Thus, in many parts of Asia and Eastern Europe, a tie-in with a local company is a prerequisite for doing business in that country. This is particularly true in countries with heavily planned economies.[18] In these instances, it is not a matter of carefully weighing the pros and cons of building your own factory or acquiring an existing one versus teaming up with a local company. Formal governmental directives often limit foreigners to minority own-

TABLE 5.1
U.S. Manufacturing Investment Abroad, 1988–1990:
Strategic Alliances and Other Options

Target Country	Acquisitions	Strategic Alliances	New Plants/ Expansions	Total
European Community	221	63	67	351
Asia	31	76	30	137
Canada	65	5	9	79
Latin America	10	14	10	34
Other Europe	27	37	3	67
Total	354	195	119	668

Source: Compiled from unpublished data sheets made available by the Conference Board, New York.

ership of local enterprises – or the power of private distribution systems may yield the same result. In Indonesia, for example, all foreign investment must be in the form of joint ventures with local partners, who eventually need to own a majority share.[19]

In contrast, in the more open economies of Canada and Western Europe (including, but not limited to, the 12 member nations of the EC), foreign companies are much freer to develop a local presence by the familiar and direct approach of acquiring a company already doing business there. It seems, at least from the data, that many firms view strategic alliances as second-best options that are only used when it is not feasible to build or buy wholly owned facilities overseas.[20] From the perspective of U.S. managers, this wariness of strategic partnerships between competitors may also be the result of periods of stringent enforcement of antitrust legislation in the United States.

The overseas strategy of the United Parcel Service (UPS) presents a cogent case in point. In its effort to dominate the international package-delivery market, UPS has acquired 12 companies in Western Europe, one of the most recent being Prost Transport of France. UPS has also bought companies in Canada, Mexico, and Australia. In the case of Japan, however, UPS has entered into a 50-50 joint venture with Yomato Transport Company to create Unistar Air Cargo. The new company is the fifth largest package carrier in Japan and also provides service between the United States and Japan.[21]

In the case of defense production, the U.S. partners may have entered some alliances only in order to gain (or avoid losing) governmental customers. Specifically, during the 1970s and 1980s, European governments demanded a greater role in the development of the military aircraft they were buying from the United States. The parallel Japanese desire to build up their aircraft manufacturing industry was exemplified by the controversial FSX fighter aircraft project, which involved a joint venture between a Japanese manufacturer and a major U.S. aerospace firm.

These demands intensified at a time when the U.S. government was eager to reduce the development costs of its weapon systems and wished to encourage standardization, especially in NATO weapons. In 1986, the U.S. Congress reinforced this trend by enacting legislation that encouraged multinational cooperation in weapons development.

Foreign governments also demanded a greater role in the production of aircraft they were purchasing from U.S. companies. Faced with the possibility that several European governments might try to develop an indigenous military fighter to rival the F-16, General Dynamics agreed to assign a major production role to domestic firms in prospective purchaser nations, including production of parts for aircraft sold to the U.S. Air Force. Aided by such arrangements, and with the backing of leading Belgian and Dutch aircraft firms, General Dynamics won the contract over strong competition.[22]

Strategic alliances are employed by firms in a wide

variety of industries. Firms with little experience in establishing formal collaborative arrangements with other companies participate in less formal partnerships. Indeed, students of strategic alliances view the core of the firm as the center of a dense web of relationships within and across industries. As some analysts note, there is an elaborate lattice of ties among organizations, some tight, some loose, which help guide an organization through an unfamiliar world.[23]

Unisys, a computer maker, is a good example of the web of alliances with which companies are typically associated. With annual sales of about $10 billion, Unisys reports that its overseas revenues – in more than 100 different countries – equal its domestic business. This enterprise is both a customer of, and a supplier to, IBM and Honeywell in the United States, BASF, Philips, and Siemens in the European Community, and Fujitsu and Hitachi in Japan. Together, these companies engage in joint ventures, coproduce, serve as sources for each other, share output, and compete.[24]

Unisys is not unique. More than one-half of Corning Glass's revenues comes from joint ventures. Two-thirds of those intercorporate undertakings are with foreign companies, including Siemens in West Germany, Ciba-Geigy in Switzerland, Plessey in the United Kingdom, Samsung in South Korea, and Asahi Glass in Japan.

Many types of strategic alliances have evolved. In some cases, the partners establish and invest in a new joint enterprise. In numerous other instances, they rely on cooperation between their existing organizational structures. Equity or ownership alliances are those in which the partners set up a separate business entity that draws on the resources of the cooperating firms and in which each partner maintains an equity position. On occasion, the firms trade or purchase equity in each other. In the case of nonownership alliances, the cooperating firms maintain their respective identities throughout the course of the joint effort. (Chapter 6 covers strategic alliances with equity investment.)

Collaborative Alliances without Equity Investment

Strategic alliances without new equity investments are partnerships in which firms pool resources while maintaining their respective identities. Ownership remains in the hands of each respective partner.

Advantages

One of the principal advantages of engaging in strategic nonequity alliances is that they give access to new or foreign markets that otherwise may be effectively closed because of the high cost of entry, governmental barriers to foreign firms, or a network of domestic enterprises that does not welcome newcomers. Alliances between companies of different nations provide opportunities to deal with whatever country has the more favorable governmental environment. Goods can be manufactured in the country with the lowest taxes, regulatory restraints, or labor costs.

Strategic alliances may be an important response to the high cost and riskiness of product development, but they are more often seen as a strategy for penetrating markets. Any number of considerations may lead a firm to consider engaging in such arrangements, however. In essence, alliances may be viewed as a means of providing the firm with a global presence when more attractive strategies are not feasible.

Flexibility is one of the main operational advantages of interfirm alliances.[25] This is particularly true for firms unable to keep up with rapidly changing consumer preferences, but which seek to meet customer demands. For instance, Dow Chemical's "preferred" supplier program and Du Pont's efforts to cooperate more closely with suppliers are efforts to meet the specific requirements and problems of their customers more effectively.[26] These newer arrangements often differ from traditional customer-supplier relations in that the supplying firms often actively participate in the design and development of new products. The firm providing a component may become responsible for the R&D work on that component under the guidance and direction of the larger company.

Moreover, unlike acquisitions or mergers, strategic alliances only need to be pursued in those parts of the participating firms' organization that will be working together.[27] Each alliance may be tailored to fit the particular requirements of each partner. Ventures to be operated jointly are determined on a project-by-project basis. Only activities that will benefit both partners—that do not require one partner to "sacrifice" for the other—are considered.[28] In this way, each company is able to maintain its independence while gaining the rewards of cooperation.

Because many firms cooperate within the same industry, collaborative ventures also allow firms to co-opt potential competitors. An especially interesting situation arises when one part of each partner cooperates while the others compete. For instance, PPG and Asahi Glass began a joint venture in Japan in 1966 to produce polyvinyl chloride. In 1985 they formed a joint automotive glass venture in the United States to compete for the business of Japanese "transplants." In 1988, they set up a chloride and caustic soda joint venture in Indonesia, along with the Mitsubishi Trading Company and local participation. During all this time, they remained global competitors in the sheet-glass business.[29] It is crucial, however, that areas of cooperation and areas of competition be clearly defined at the beginning of the partnership.[30]

By pooling resources, cooperating firms are able to spread out the risks associated with operating on a global scale. In the pharmaceutical or biotechnology area, risk is lowered by faster entry and government certification, the result of swapping the technology and clinical testing data of the principals of the venture.[31] For example, G. D. Searle & Co. and Hokuriku Seiyaku Co. have worked together since 1987. Hokuriku granted Searle a worldwide license to sell some of its pharmaceuticals, while the Japanese firm is a conduit for selling many of the U.S. firm's products in

Japan.[32] It is the risk-sharing nature of strategic alliances that often produces the incentive for cooperating firms to engage in and remain committed to the alliance.[33]

Disadvantages

Although strategic alliances are often effective forms of business relationships, the many failures in attempted ventures should not be ignored. This is particularly true considering the oft-cited figure that 7 out of every 10 alliances "fail." It is important to note, however, that although some alliances do in fact end in "failure," many partnerships are dissolved because the cooperative venture has reached fruition.[34]

Cooperation is a more difficult and often a less desirable option than independent expansion because of the complexities involved and the management qualities demanded.[35] When strategic alliances fail, it is typically because partnerships can be more difficult to manage or control than other forms of business operations, such as wholly owned facilities overseas. Partnerships often involve the merger of different, and sometimes conflicting, corporate cultures, as well as different technological capabilities, which may lead to slower and more complex decision making.[36]

An analysis of responses from 11,678 business leaders around the world revealed that the companies of most respondents are engaged in at least a few joint ventures or alliances. The more joint venture experience they have, however, the more they identify managerial issues, such as loss of control and information, as worrisome. Those with less experience consider that the biggest risks involve political and macroeconomic factors such as exchange rates.[37]

Moreover, alliances that are not properly structured for the particular venture are also prone to failure. This is particularly important for alliances between traditionally strong competitors and for partnerships in which the advantages to one partner are not balanced by the advantages of the other. To be successful for an extended period of time, a relative balance of benefits between the partners is necessary, as well as a balance of risks shared by each partner. If one partner feels taken advantage of, the alliance is bound to fail.[38]

Thomas C. MacAvoy, vice chairman of Corning Glass, states this position very succinctly: "If I tried to gain the upper hand in a joint venture, my boss would reprimand me. We want to establish a feeling of mutuality and trust."[39] In this spirit, Corning seeks partners with compatible values and cultures, presses for 50-50 ownership, and sets the venture apart from both parents.

A further important disadvantage often associated with nonequity alliances is the potential for partners to misappropriate proprietary knowledge or sensitive technologies existing before the formation of the alliance or developed as a result of the cooperative venture. Many in the United States worry, as we saw earlier, that cooperation between General Dynamics and Mitsubishi Heavy Industries in their efforts to jointly develop the FSX advanced jet fighter will give the Japanese the technology necessary to compete with the United States in the next generation of commercial and military aircraft products.[40]

R&D Cooperatives and Technology Swaps

Alliances based on the cooperation of firms engaging in R&D differ from those in which firms share existing technologies, although the nature of each alliance is essentially similar. In particular, R&D agreements involve the cooperation of firms either in the design and development of new technologies or in the improvement of existing technologies. Participating firms may thus contribute financing, technological skills, and equipment or other assets, as well as access to large or international markets when R&D leads to the production of new products.[41] In 1991, for example, United Technologies and General Electric, along with Britain's Rolls-Royce and France's SNECMA, signed up to participate in a Japanese-funded project to develop a new supersonic aircraft engine.[42]

Technology swaps, on the other hand, are similar to the licensing agreements discussed in chapter 3, although they usually do not involve the "sale" or transfer of technological know-how for money. Instead, technology swaps are usually trades of technology for technology. In many instances, however, such alliances regularly entail a combination of both R&D and technology swapping.

The number of cooperative R&D alliances has increased significantly since the early 1970s. Although precise figures are not available, there is some indication that between 1973 and 1988, cooperative R&D ventures and technology-sharing arrangements increased as much as 13-fold.[43] The largest number of agreements were in information technology and new materials. Companies in the United States, Europe, and Japan entered into more cooperative ventures with foreign enterprises than with firms in their home countries.[44]

The alliance between AT&T and NEC of Japan is a good example of the nature of many R&D and technology-sharing partnerships. AT&T traded some of its proprietary computer-aided design technology in return for advanced logic chips designs developed by NEC. In addition, both companies agreed to share the basic technologies on how to manufacture semiconductors as well as cooperate in the development of more advanced semiconductor technologies.[45] Philips, the Dutch producer of consumer electronics, has cooperated extensively with Matsushita of Japan in developing new products such as compact discs and VCRs.[46]

These are hardly isolated examples. Sweden's Volvo and France's Renault have also established a strategic alliance, with an explicit division of labor. Renault is doing diesel-engine development, while Volvo is handling advanced emissions controls. The two enterprises are also moving to coordinate parts purchasing, transportation and communication, and new-product strategy.[47] An interesting variation is the collaboration between the U.S. firm Digital Equipment Corporation and Italy's Olivetti & Co. The two companies are funding and sharing the results from Olivetti's research laboratory in Cambridge, England.[48]

A more limited R&D alliance is that between Texas Instruments and Hitachi, in which the two firms agreed to combine efforts over a 10-year period to design advanced computer memory chips. By teaming up in this project, each company can explore more technology paths than it could alone. Yet both firms can reduce the R&D investment needed to develop the new technology. The agreement is limited to the R&D phase, however, because Texas Instruments is a participant in Sematech, the U.S. consortium that is developing new manufacturing technologies not intended to be shared with foreign companies.[49]

Boeing, General Electric, McDonnell Douglas, and United Technologies are all participating in an unprecedented international cooperative arrangement to design a second-generation commercial supersonic aircraft. The new plane is likely to be so expensive that no one company is willing to invest all of the funds needed for the exploratory developmental phase.

Boeing and McDonnell Douglas are working with three European partners—British Aerospace, France's Aerospatiale, and Deutsche Airbus of Germany—in estimating market potential and dealing with environmental issues, such as ground noise, sonic boom, and emissions. General Electric and Pratt & Whitney are cooperating with Britain's Rolls-Royce and France's SNECMA to develop quieter, more economical, and clean-burning engines. At a later time, the companies will decide whether to produce the plane jointly or create competing versions.[50]

The Decision to Engage in Joint
R & D or Technology Alliances

Generally, businesses enter into technology-sharing relationships with the intention of pooling resources and sharing the high costs associated with advances in technological development. Because firms rarely know beforehand the nature of the products that are likely to be developed as a result of R&D, however, and because the future profitability of new technology is usually uncertain, the risk when potential competitors cooperate in R&D is significant.

This risk has three primary sources. First, there is the possibility that the R&D or cross-licensing efforts will not produce marketable products. Second, the extent to which potential products will be demanded may be unclear, especially for the introduction of new products. Third, the action taken by competitors, especially if a competitor is an alliance partner, may be uncertain as well.[51]

Reasons to Engage in Technology Alliances.   R&D cooperatives or technology swaps are effective strategies when R&D costs for individual firms are very high, thus leading firms to share costs and risks. Indeed, many see joint R&D efforts as the direct result of the spiraling costs of research.[52] Consequently, development alliances are most often observed in mature, yet fast changing, high-tech industries, such as electronics, telecommunications, and robotics.[53]

For instance, IBM has established an alliance with Germany's Siemens to research next-generation megabyte memory chips because R&D in new sophisticated technologies, such as advanced computer chips, is expensive when carried out separately by independent firms. Some observers believe that such cooperative ventures point the way toward the future.[54]

R&D alliances are also optimal when research is focused on technologies that are not easily licensed.[55] When technology is rapidly changing, firms may find it necessary to transfer the technology into marketable products as quickly as possible to maximize expected profits before the product's technology becomes obsolete. A firm often accomplishes this by licensing the production and marketing of the technology or product to companies in several different markets. When the technology is not easily licensed, cooperation with other firms in its development may be more effective because partners could cooperate in the production and marketing of the product without needing to develop complicated licensing agreements with other businesses.

As in licensing agreements, firms often engage in technology swaps or joint R&D projects when each company wants access to technology and technical know-how possessed by the other firm, as in the case of AT&T and NEC. Another example is a venture involving the development of the V2500 turbofan jet engine, for which Pratt & Whitney and Rolls-Royce integrated complementary technologies. Pratt & Whitney concentrated on the development of the hot-section technology, and Rolls-Royce developed the fan and compressor sections.[56]

Restrictions on the transfer of technology between partners, however, particularly from a technologically advanced to a "junior" firm, may make collaboration appear less desirable. Development of the CFM56, the jet aircraft engine produced by the General Electric–SNECMA joint venture, was delayed a year because the U.S. Department of Defense opposed the transfer of the engine core compressor technology to a foreign firm. Consequently, GE was required to ship the compressor in a sealed "black box" for installation by SNECMA engineers. In addition, SNECMA had to agree to make royalty payments to the U.S. government for each engine the joint venture partnership produced because the compressor was developed by GE with public funds. Although the GE–SNECMA partnership is considered successful, other partners in similar alliances may consider a subcontracting role preferable.[57]

Reasons for Not Engaging in Technology Alliances. Technology alliances are not particularly useful when a company does not wish to share proprietary technical material outside the firm—especially when such knowledge might fuel a potential competitor. This reluctance to share arouses the greatest concern in most R&D partnerships,[58] especially in highly competitive industries, where monetary rewards typically follow the companies that introduce products before their competitors – the so-called first move advantage. This situation also underscores the fact that instability and mistrust are a fundamental barrier cooperating competitors must overcome to ensure a successful alliance.

R&D cooperatives are not effective when the proposed R&D cooperative is not expected to exhibit economies of scale. In these cases it may be better for the firm to centralize R&D within its own organization, or at least at one location, rather than pursue it at several places around the world.[59] If it appears that R&D efforts will improve when conducted at one location instead of several, partners may decide to concentrate R&D at one firm. The other firm may then finance the developmental projects in return for the licensing or production rights of the new technology.

Joint Production and Marketing Agreements

Joint production agreements, also known as coproduction agreements, are similar in key ways to subcontracting and to joint ventures. All three approaches often entail the licensing of specialized components or the joint construction and operation of facilities or business units. Coproducing partners are, however, typically more closely involved in the development of the product to be produced than is the case in conventional subcontracting. Unlike equity alliances, assets and management are not combined into a distinct business entity when firms agree to produce or distribute jointly. Although joint production alliances may require devoting a substantial amount of resources to the venture, the joint activity is often less formally structured than traditional joint ventures.

Some cross-border partnerships serve several purposes. For example, the development of a new model jet airliner is a very expensive proposition, stretching the financial ability of the largest firms in the industry. In addition, foreign governments are reluctant to see their airlines pay in essence for the development of technology in another nation.

Cross-border alliances are a method for dealing with both issues. In the case of Boeing's new 777 commercial jet airliner, companies in six different nations are partners in the development and production work. They share the financial burden and acquire some of the technology. Boeing's international partners include

- Alenia (formerly Aeritalia) of Italy, for the outboard wing flaps
- Aerospace Technologies of Australia, for the rudder
- Mitsubishi, Kawasaki, and Fuji of Japan, for the fuselage panels and doors, and the wing ribs
- Korean Air, for the flap covers
- Menasco Aerospace of Canada, for the landing gears
- General Electric of Britain, for the primary flight computers.[60]

Coproduction is one of the most common forms of interfirm cooperation among Western firms doing business in Asia and Eastern Europe. Traditionally, this was due to the fact that countries behind the Iron Curtain discouraged foreign ownership of local companies.[61]

In addition to their attractiveness when other forms of alliances are not permitted, joint production or marketing agreements are useful to achieve the economies of scale and scope associated with the pooling of resources in the production process. Again, this approach is often found in industries in which product technology is changing rapidly and in which manufacturers are forced to shorten the product development cycle.

In the computer industry, new semiconductor technology results in improvements in microprocessor performance on an average of 50 percent every year. Similarly, data storage capacity increases approximately 100 percent annually, while memory density improves as much as 400 percent every three years. In addition, product life cycles have shortened to three years, from an average of seven years.[62] By jointly producing and marketing products, firms are often able to substantially reduce the costs and risks associated with the manufacturing of high-tech products.

Companies often enter into coproduction alliances at the invitation of foreign companies. South Korean aerospace companies have negotiated with United Technologies' Sikorsky Aircraft and McDonnell Douglas for the licensed coproduction of the UH-60A Black Hawk helicopters and the F/A-18 strike fighter aircraft respectively. Initially, kits are supplied by the U.S. firms for assembly in the Republic of Korea. Later, however, the Korean companies will probably develop and manufacture the aircraft in greater detail.[63]

Joint marketing alliances are similar to joint production agreements, except they involve the distribution of the product after it has been produced. Characteristic joint marketing alliances include agricultural cooperatives in the United States, which advertise and lobby as a single group on behalf of agricultural firms, as well as more formal distribution enterprises put together by local businesses and foreign manufacturers desiring to enter an overseas market.

Joint marketing arrangements are numerous. In automobiles, Nissan distributes Volkswagens in Japan; Volkswagen sells Nissan's four-wheel-drive cars in Europe. In pharmaceuticals, Marion-Merrill-Dow distributes Tanabe's Herbesser and Chugai's Ulcerim in the United States, while Merck markets Yamanouchi's Gaster, and Eli Lilly sells Fujisawa's Cefamezin. In Japan, Shionogi distributes Lilly's Ceclor as Kefral. Sankyo distributes Squibb's Capoten; Takeda, Bayer's Adalat; and Fujisawa, SmithKline's Tagamet.[64]

Strategic alliances in the area of marketing are also used by service firms. For example, the insurance services firm Alexander & Alexander maintains correspondent relationships with Peltours Insurance Agencies of Israel, All Risk Norway, and Aegis Insurance Company of Greece.[65]

The Decision to Engage in Joint
Production or Marketing Alliances

Because joint production or marketing agreements are often similar in nature to joint ventures and subcontracting agreements, the considerations that participating firms take into account are in general also very similar. Nevertheless, several special issues arise, among them whether to form a separate business entity.

A joint production venture without equity can be especially useful at an initial stage of a partnership that may be expected to grow into a long-term relationship.[66] Firms may decide to "try out" the alliance to assess its potential effectiveness. If both partners believe that the alliance meets the objectives of each company, a more extensive alliance can be formed involving joint equity control. For the most part, the decision regarding the use of joint production or joint marketing alliances depends on how long the relationship is expected to last.

Informal Alliances

Informal alliances are cooperative associations between firms that are more casual in nature than the agreements that we have been examining. They do not dramatically affect a company's organizational structure or competitive position.[67] Typically they include discussions between management or technical personnel regarding potentially more extensive strategic partnerships.

The Decision to Participate in Informal Alliances

Informal alliances are quite common among firms in all industries. They are useful when risks are small and when mutual trust exists between partners. For instance, the heads of the computer software giants Microsoft and

Ashton-Tate have maintained a friendship over the years, occasionally discussing the state of their industry. This is in spite of the fact that both companies compete heavily.[68]

Furthermore, informal alliances are effective for promoting "discussions" on solving problems or as a good starting point for more formal arrangements. The alliance between IBM and Apple Computer was the result of less formal discussions between representatives of both companies. Firms may also engage in informal alliances when a firm considers itself weak or a runner-up and thus wishes to avoid precipitating aggressive moves by its competitors.[69] Informal alliances are also useful when a firm is interested in cooperation without visibility. This is usually the case when a firm wishes to establish a position or test a relationship before a more formal, visible alliance emerges.

Informal alliances are not particularly appropriate when the potential relationship is complex and long term and when rapid change is expected or desired.[70] Although informal alliances are useful as a first step leading to more extensive strategic partnerships, they may not be appropriate if the alliance is expected or planned to become more complicated. This is particularly true if the partnership is beginning to involve significant financial commitments. In this case a firm may prefer to formalize the relationship, perhaps by entering into a joint venture or joint production agreement.

Conclusion

The nature of cross-border alliances has undergone a veritable metamorphosis in recent years. In the past, an alliance typically involved a trade-off, with one partner providing industrial know-how or new technology in return for a guaranteed position in the other's market. Often the junior partner in this arrangement acted as a subcontractor on an existing line or, slightly upscale, as a licensed producer.

Increasingly, alliances are taking a more forward-looking approach. They typically begin at the front end, with joint development of new products and markets. These interfirm arrangements are far more likely to involve a real sharing of technology and the financial risk that goes with it. The speed of development becomes a more important competitive factor.

The aerospace industry provides a cogent example. McDonnell Douglas first established a relationship with Alenia of Italy more than 25 years ago. At first, the Italian firm supplied parts for the U.S. company's line of commercial aircraft. Now, Alenia is working on joint development of a new radar-equipped version of the AV–8B Harrier II (a VTOL, or vertical take-off and landing aircraft). The project also involves British Aerospace (the creator of the Harrier I) and CASA of Spain.[71]

Forming strategic alliances with potential competitors is an extremely difficult and delicate activity. From 1987 to 1989, McDonnell Douglas was engaged in ultimately unsuccessful discussions with Europe's Airbus Industries—the consortium of companies located in several different European countries—on the development of new commercial aircraft. The two firms are now engaged in head-to-head competition in that market.

As we have seen, strategic alliances can be an effective way for domestically oriented firms to respond to the global marketplace. Indeed, interfirm cooperation seems to be the emerging pattern in high-cost, high-tech markets and when firms endeavor to spread out the costs of development and production. They are also important in markets that restrict more direct approaches to operating overseas, such as exporting or investing in a wholly owned subsidiary.

Strategic alliances are flexible and often transitional arrangements, even those that involve outright formation of new enterprises. Many are also expected to lead to enduring links between partners. At times, however, other intercompany arrangements can be superior in meeting the needs of the corporation. In any event, an examination of nonequity strategic alliances shows that they yield attractive potential advantages as well as serious and often costly disadvantages.

6

Strategic Alliances with Equity Investment

When companies decide that strategic alliances are an effective means of operating within a global marketplace, they must grapple with questions about the nature of ownership and control within the alliance. Should the partnership be limited to the contribution of resources or know-how? Should a more substantial equity investment be made by each partner? These important issues involve more than simply determining how responsibilities and rewards are to be divided between partners. Difficult managerial and legal problems also arise, such as how decisions will be made and how conflicts will be resolved.

Chapter 5 discussed the nature of strategic alliances in general and, in particular, those alliances that do not involve the joint ownership of the venture itself. This chapter examines cooperative alliances in which the partnership is based on ownership rather than merely cooperation.

Collaborative Alliances with Equity Investment

The distinguishing characteristic of collaborative alliances involving ownership is that each participating firm has an invested equity stake in the partnership. This is in contrast to other alliances in which firms contribute machinery, technical know-how, or even money to the partnership but do not directly participate in a joint ownership structure.

The automotive industry is a good example of alliances in which an equity investment plays an important role in the partnership. It also illustrates, as seen in figure 6.1, the complex web of alliances among firms.

For instance, General Motors owns 40 percent of Isuzu and 5 percent of Suzuki; Ford and Nissan are jointly developing a new minivan; Ford also operates a joint venture with Volkswagen in Brazil and owns 25 percent of Mazda; Nissan owns 5 percent of Subaru's producer, Fuji Heavy Industries.[1]

Advantages

One of the primary advantages of ownership alliances is that they allow entry into markets otherwise restricted by governmental regulations or other barriers. This is particularly true for joint ventures, as will be shown below.

Most direct foreign investment in Eastern Europe is in the form of joint ventures or ownership alliances. In Hungary, General Motors owns two-thirds of Raba, an automobile production operation, and General Electric owns three-fourths of Tungsram, a light bulb producer. In Poland, Beloit Company has an 80 percent interest in Fampa, a paper machinery production enterprise, and Gerber Products has a 60 percent stake in Alima, the country's largest baby food manufacturer. Dow has purchased a 51 percent interest in Czechoslovakia's Chemicke Zavody Sokolov, a producer of acrylic acid and acrylic ester. Most of the output is used by Dow in making paints, adhesives, and absorbent layers for disposable diapers. Chevron Corporation and the government of Kazakhstan, in the former Soviet Union, have entered into a 50-50 joint venture to develop the Tengiz oil field. One of the few exceptions is Procter and Gamble's 100 percent ownership of Rakona, a cleaning business in Czechoslovakia.[2]

FIGURE 6.1
Equity Alliances in the Automobile Industry

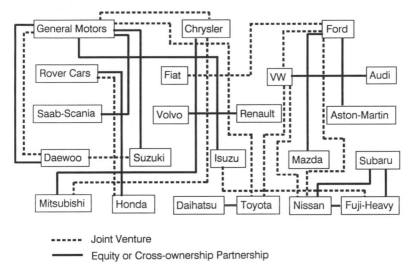

Source: Center for the Study of American Business, Washington University.

Several Western firms have entered into joint ventures with military enterprises in the former Soviet Union. For example, Gillette has entered into a deal with the Leninetz military complex to manufacture 750 million razor blades a year. Gulfstream Aerospace Corporation is working with the Sukhoi Design Bureau to build a supersonic corporate jet. The Pratt and Whitney division of United Technologies has entered into an arrangement with the Tupolev Aviation Corporation to develop large passenger aircraft.

The Coca-Cola Company has made an initial investment of $12 million in a joint venture with the city of Moscow to produce and sell Coke products in Russia. Known as Coca-Cola Refreshments-Moscow, the new enterprise is setting up a syrup-producing plant in Solntsevo and a network of about 2,000 kiosks in Moscow.[3]

These joint ventures have several attractions to the

companies in the capitalist nations. They represent an opportunity to enter a new market with minimum risk. For defense contractors, such deals are an offset to the declining domestic military market. Moreover, the military sector of the Soviet Union traditionally had the nation's best managers, most advanced technology, and most disciplined work force. The Russian partners view Western firms as more than an important source of capital. They are expected to provide levels of quality control that will keep Russian consumers from buying preferred, albeit higher priced, imports.[4]

Like strategic alliances in general, ownership alliances have the advantage of minimizing the risks inherent in a fast-changing, growing world economy. The nature of the risk reduction in equity alliances, however, is somewhat different from other forms of alliances. This is because each equity partner is more closely linked to the success of the venture, each having a vested ownership position in the venture itself.

Another advantage of equity alliances is that the costs borne by each partner are often lower than the direct investment costs incurred in establishing production facilities overseas or participating in other forms of strategic partnership. This is true for ownership alliances that form when firms acquire an equity stake in another firm, as in joint equity swaps. For every foreign company operating in Eastern Europe, the purchase or joint operation of an existing plant was far less hazardous than the establishment of a new production facility.

Cross-border equity partnerships also bring significant benefits to the local partners, thus ensuring a more stable and lasting relationship. These benefits may include upgrading technology and marketing skills, introducing modern management techniques, and providing jobs to local workers. In the case of Eastern Europe, foreign firms can help in a more basic way: they can show local companies how to move from nationalized enterprises under Communist rule to industrial businesses that can compete in the commercial marketplace.

Disadvantages

These equity partnerships often generate lower growth potential than other global strategies, such as direct acquisitions of overseas production facilities. Firms that use a combination of approaches, however, such as joint venture with a cross-licensing agreement, are usually more profitable than those that do not.[5]

The formation of strategic alliances such as joint ventures usually requires complex and detailed contracts delineating the precise nature of the venture. This may be especially true between countries with vastly different cultural or social norms.[6] The importance of complex, detailed contracts in the development of joint ventures with U.S. companies may also be the result of the domination of business negotiation by lawyers.

Similarly, equity alliances are often difficult to manage. Organization cultures or management styles may differ among participating firms, especially between U.S. and foreign companies. American firms generally want to shape and control the decision-making process, at times causing potential partners to back away. During the 1950s and 1960s, U.S. manufacturing dominated joint arrangements as U.S. technology flowed to foreign firms. Today, many foreign companies are more evenly matched with the United States and want a greater role in project development.

In the words of an analysis by the U.S. aerospace industry's own trade association, "past U.S. attitudes persist." Some U.S. companies apparently undertake international cooperative ventures with the belief that there is nothing their partner company can teach them. It seems clear that U.S. firms can learn much by adopting the very different attitude of their Asian counterparts: assimilate as much knowledge and experience from your foreign partners as you can and then adapt what is useful to your own operations.[7]

Equity partnerships may also result in difficulties when the deal to create the alliance is such that the interests of the local partner conflict with the global strategies of the other firm. For instance, the alliance between General Motors and Daewoo of South Korea went sour when Daewoo's desire to expand in local markets conflicted with its partner's more global objectives.[8]

Many other problems arose in that star-crossed relationship. In theory, the General Motors–Daewoo Group marriage should have been ideal. The U.S. automotive giant would combine the engineering done at its German subsidiary with low-cost Korean labor and American marketing know-how to produce a competitive, low-priced, subcompact car. The joint venture, Daewoo Motor, would yield a truly global product.

The managers of the two companies clashed frequently, however. They seriously underestimated the obstacles posed by their three-continent arrangement. When problems arose in the German-designed braking systems, GM engineers in Europe experienced great difficulty in translating their design changes so that Korean suppliers and assemblers could follow them.

When Daewoo negotiated a sale of 7,000 automobiles in Eastern Europe, GM executives were outraged: Europe was a market assigned to GM's Opel subsidiary. Daewoo Shipbuilding (a sister organization of Daewoo Motor) is now building a minicar with Japan's Suzuki Motor Company. General Motors is expected to sell Daewoo Group its 50 percent stake in their joint venture.[9]

Special difficulties arise in the transitional economies of Eastern Europe and the republics of the former Soviet Union. The situation has been likened to a "Yukon–Wild West economy," where investors do not know for sure if they have legal title to the items they purchase or recourse to a body of commercial law to support them. As a result, of the more than 2,000 deals between Americans and authorities in Russia and the other republics recorded by the U.S. Department of Commerce, only about 50 were functioning as of late 1991.[10]

Similarly, rapidly changing economic conditions may also present problems for some alliances. For instance, the highly touted GE-Tungsian joint venture in Hungary was forced to stop production and new investment for several weeks. The suspensions were attributed to unanticipated losses resulting from 30 percent annual inflation and small devaluations in the Hungarian currency.[11]

Equity alliances come in various forms: joint ventures, joint equity swaps, affiliates, satellite enterprises, minority investment alliances, and minority affiliates. Joint ventures are partnerships in which the combination of resources from the participating firms results in a separate business entity. Joint equity swaps are alliances in which each firm exchanges ownership in the other. Affiliations, satellite enterprises, and minority equity partnerships are similar to joint equity swaps although, instead of trading equity stakes, the partnership typically consists of one company taking some form of equity position in the other firm.

Joint Ventures

Joint ventures are equity or ownership alliances that usually result in the formation of a separate corporate entity jointly run under a different name. Many examples abound. GMF Robotics is the robotics manufacturer jointly operated by General Motors and Fanuc Ltd. of Japan. The partnership between General Electric and SNECMA of France, called CFM International, was set up to develop and manufacture jet aircraft engines.

Most joint ventures are usually governed by a board representing the contributing partners. The legal form of the new organization may be a contract, a corporation, an unincorporated association or another legal entity.[12]

Joint ventures often take a variety of forms. For instance, a company may join with a foreign firm to operate in its home market and export (or sell domestically). Himont, the world's largest producer of polypropylene, was a highly successful joint venture formed in 1983 between Hercules in the United States and Montedison of Italy.[13] Corning

Glass and Plessey Company of England jointly operate PlessLor Optronics Inc., a producer of fiber optic devices.

Alternatively, the company may join with a foreign firm and run the venture in the foreign market. Iwaki Glass, a producer of television bulk glass and other consumer products based in Japan, is a joint venture between Corning Glass and Asahi Glass of Japan. Boeing and the Saudi Arabian national airline, together with other Saudi companies, have formed a joint venture called the Al-Salam Aircraft Company. The new company is building nine aircraft hangars in Saudi Arabia to provide maintenance facilities for civil and military jets.[14]

Also, the company may join with a foreign firm and operate the joint venture in a third nation. Autolatina, the South American auto producer, is a joint venture between Ford in the United States and Volkswagen of Germany.

John Deere has joined up with Italy's Fiat and Japan's Hitachi in a venture to make construction equipment in Europe. The new venture is designed to compete against Caterpillar, which has factories in Belgium and France, and Komatsu, with plants in Britain and Germany.[15]

GTE heads a consortium that includes AT&T and Telefonia Internationale de España to run the Venezuela telephone system. The consortium holds a 40 percent stake in the state telephone company and will have broad managerial control. From the viewpoint of Venezuela, the entry of high-tech foreign companies responds to widespread criticism of poor service and outdated equipment. GTE views the venture as a way of carrying out its strategy of seeking international opportunities to complement its strong but slow-growing domestic telecommunications business.[16]

There are many variations on the theme of matching one firm's desire for geographic diversification with a foreign firm's need for a partner with high technology, modern management techniques, and substantial capital. A joint venture between General Motors Europe and a state-owned automobile maker in Poland plans to produce cars that will be sold domestically. The joint venture, the result of one of the largest investments in Poland by a Western company, will give GM majority control and access to the Polish market. In return for the inflow of Western capital, technology, and expertise, GM will be allowed to import into Poland a portion of its models duty free.[17]

A different type of joint venture is the transatlantic high-capacity fiber optic cable being built by America's MCI and British Telecommunications. The cable will be used by both companies, each of which serve basically different but complementary markets.

Other producers of telecommunications equipment are also entering into numerous international joint ventures. IBM and Germany's Siemens each own half of Rolm Company, a supplier of office phone switching equipment. Siecor, the joint venture between Corning Glass and Siemens, is one of the largest U.S. producers of fiber optic cable. Motorola has established a technology partnership with Canada's Northern Telecom to shore up its position in the cellular network market.[18]

Pacific Telesis is a 26 percent participant in a major joint venture led by Mannesmann to provide mobile telephone service in Germany. The U.S. firm is handling the bulk of the design and engineering. Other partners include Britain's Cable & Wireless, Deutsche Genossenschafts Bank, and Lyonnaise des Eaux. Pacific Telesis also holds a 23 percent stake in Telecel, an international consortium that is building a cellular phone system in Portugal. It will compete with a network operated by Telecom Portugal, a joint venture of the two state-owned companies.

In 1991, Bell Atlantic, the U.S telecommunications company, sold a half interest in its own operation in Western Europe to International Computers Ltd., the 80 percent owned British unit of Fujitsu. The justification given was to enhance marketing clout. Bell Atlantic and U.S. West share a 49 percent interest in building and operating a mobile telephone and data transmission network in Czechoslovakia. The local partner is the Post and Telecommunications Administrations of the Czech and Slovak Republic.[19]

In the fall of 1991, IBM announced a cooperation agreement with BT, formerly British Telecommunications, aimed at helping companies cope with the mounting complexities of modern telecommunications. The venture, Syncordia, is based on the premise that multinational companies will increasingly want to contract out their telecommunications activities, especially as borders open across the European continent.

Syncordia will focus on the 400 to 500 multinational companies with about $1 billion or more in annual revenue. An ideal customer would be an airline with offices in a dozen countries facing a dozen different regulatory systems and a dozen different configurations in computer gear. BT will provide its Concert management system and IBM its Netview software to form a sophisticated alarm and repair system for the airline's far-flung operations.[20]

International joint ventures have been growing rapidly since the early 1980s. In 1983, Business International identified 55 cross-border alliances and joint projects, including 9 liaisons between U.S. and Japanese companies, 32 between U.S. and EC firms, and 8 between Japanese and EC enterprises. Within the EC, there were six joint ventures between companies from different European countries.

Three years later, the pattern changed markedly as the single market integration began. The number of joint ventures between U.S. and European companies was up 50 percent, as were those between U.S. and Japanese firms. No change occurred in the annual number of joint ventures between EC and Japanese firms. In contrast, there was an almost eightfold increase in international joint ventures within the EC, from 6 in 1983 to 46 in 1986. By 1989, cross-border joint ventures became so numerous in the EC (well into the hundreds) that precise data are no longer available.[21]

Joint ventures have now become a standard approach for interfirm business relations. As economic growth slows and industries in the United States, Europe, and Japan

mature, markets become crowded. Simultaneously, technological change accelerates to speeds at which individual
firms cannot recover their initial investments alone. A new
attitude of cooperation typically becomes necessary. The
new willingness of managers to contemplate cooperative
strategies represents a watershed in their way of thinking.[22]

In some cases, joint ventures are simply transitional
arrangements, associated with the gradual spinning off of
an existing plant to a new owner. That many joint ventures
last only a limited time does not necessarily mean that they
have failed in their purpose. The original intent on the part
of the partners may have been to deal with a temporary
market condition or a product with limited life. In other
cases, however, joint ventures are expected to establish enduring links between partners.[23]

The Decision to Engage in Joint Ventures

Many analysts believe that joint ventures will be increasingly important in the development of new industries and
the revitalization of mature ones. Often the motives for
joint ventures are not primarily monetary but instead involve learning, market entry, acquisition of capital or technology, and the facilitation of regulatory dealings.[24]

Yet, by their nature, they are often unstable and difficult
to manage, being most useful during periods of transition.
Observation of current management practices suggests am-
bivalence concerning the use of this strategy, which involves
sharing both capital and risk. Thus, because of the unique
nature of cooperation when equity investments are involved,
decisions to engage in joint ventures are based on different
criteria than are other strategic alliances.

Reasons to Engage in Joint Ventures.   Joint ventures
are particularly appropriate when complementary needs exist between firms and when the partners' strategies are
compatible.[25] This ensures that the participating companies
maintain a reasonable and effective degree of cooperation

and commitment throughout the life of the agreement. The oft-cited venture between General Motors and Toyota (New United Motor Manufacturing Incorporated or NUMMI) developed because GM brought to it a U.S. distribution network and Toyota contributed small car designs and improved manufacturing methods. It enabled Toyota to try out various hiring and training strategies with employees unionized by the United Auto Workers and General Motors to learn about key management practices.[26]

Joint ventures are especially useful when projects involve costly technological innovations or high information costs. They can also be effective when a firm wants to expand into a field or market that is alien to it. Thus, multinational enterprises have established sales affiliates with local distribution companies as partners. Similarly, joint ventures are also appropriate when a firm wants to take advantage of a local enterprise's connections or knowledge.[27]

Furthermore, as with many strategic alliances, joint ventures may be necessary when the host government's policies restrict whole ownership or other forms of direct investment strategy. Many Pacific Rim countries, such as Indonesia and Thailand, often require, or at least strongly encourage, foreign investors to form joint ventures with local partners. That helps to ensure that domestic companies share the profits as well as gain access to foreign technology and managerial expertise. Similarly, joint ventures are typically the preferred strategy for operating in nations in which the local currency is not convertible, as in the former Soviet Union.[28]

U.S. companies are much more concerned with obtaining majority ownership in an overseas joint venture than are Japanese firms. Such a concern for control may be a serious impediment to continued and successful partnerships with foreign companies, especially when the alliances are crucial to maintaining a presence in a desired market. According to the head of a major Singapore enterprise (who formerly headed IBM's operations in that nation), "The question of ownership never comes up when we're dealing with Japanese companies. It's kind of considered rude to ask for 51%. That's just not the way we, or the Japanese, do business."[29]

Many U.S. corporations insist on obtaining majority ownership of joint ventures for several very logical reasons. First of all, the parent firm can consolidate the financial performance of the venture with its own financial statements only when the stake is more than 50 percent. The Foreign Corrupt Practices Act is another factor. Majority ownership supposedly enables the U.S. partner to control the behavior of the joint venture and thus avoid running afoul of the detailed provisions of the statute. Japanese firms, in contrast, are more likely to see their relationship as two-sided, with each partner bringing substantial worth to the venture.

In addition, when a host country is growing rapidly, a joint venture may be the most effective strategy because it gives the entering firm the advantage of working with a partner knowledgeable about the local market. Consequently, the partnership might be more flexible and responsive to changes within the market than if the U.S. company were to attempt to operate alone. Moreover, the partnership may be able to take advantage of local changes quickly because joint ventures are a little more distanced from the outside company's headquarters.[30]

Finally, joint ventures are appropriate for mature industries in which excess capacity exists. Thus, the need for restructuring is met by rationalizing production and reducing output levels within the context of the cooperative agreement. Ultimately, strategic alliances are based on mutual need. Mutual need, in turn, creates tension and conflict. But, if managed well, these demanding relationships can be the basis for a formidable competitive advantage.[31]

Reasons for Avoiding Joint Ventures. A joint venture may not be particularly appropriate if intangible assets are involved (for example, trademarks, patents, managerial information, or reputation). In these cases, a licensing or

franchising arrangement may be more effective. If a technological edge is necessary to maintain competitiveness, joint
ventures may weaken a firm's ability to innovate and respond to changes in the market. If it is possible, 100 percent ownership allows firms greater control over the use of
the technological assets and permits greater control over
quality.[32]

Firms entering partnerships that they anticipate will
be long term in nature may be better off developing a more
solidified relationship, as in a joint equity swap or even
merger. Joint ventures are typically used for one particular
activity; the synergies developed are exhausted over a finite
time period. As a result, the venture is subsequently dissolved or it may be discontinued by one partner buying out
the other.[33] As with joint production agreements discussed
earlier, however, joint ventures may be useful as a means of
"testing out" the relationship before moving on to more
elaborate partnerships.

Just as the number of cross-border joint ventures has
been rising, so have the terminations of these arrangements.
Du Pont and Philips of the Netherlands ended their cooperative agreement because of different goals, as did Borden and
Meiji Milk Products of Japan.[34] The cross-border failures are
by no means limited to U.S. partners. In 1975, Bull (France),
Siemens (Germany), and Philips (Netherlands) abandoned the
first serious attempt to form a Europe-based computer alliance, Unidata. A second attempt, involving Bull and Olivetti,
was vetoed by the French government.[35]

McKinsey & Co. studied the cross-border alliances of
150 top companies, 50 each in the United States, Japan,
and Europe. They concluded that alliances between strong
and weak firms rarely work. Alliances with uneven splits of
financial ownership are also less likely to succeed. Acquisitions work better for core businesses and for expansions in
geographic areas in which the company already operates. In
any event, many alliances are only temporary. More than 75
percent of the alliances that terminated were acquired by
one of the parents.[36]

Joint Equity Swaps, Affiliates, and Other Investment Alliances

Joint equity swaps, minority investment alliances, and affiliates are similar to joint ventures in that they involve some form of cooperative co-ownership association between two or more firms. Typically, they are associations in which one firm takes an equity position in another, usually obtaining less than majority ownership. Unlike a joint venture, a joint equity swap or affiliate will not result in the formation of a separate business entity. Thus, equity partnerships are usually characterized by a decision for two or more companies to exchange shares or combine operations for a strategic purpose, such as establishing a long-term commitment of cooperation and growth.

The exchange of equity between two or more firms is not the same as the acquisition of another company or the merger of two or more enterprises. Investment alliances, such as joint equity swaps, allow partners to maintain separate identities to a significant degree.

Trading equity shares or acquiring stakes in another company are typically motivated by similar strategies. At times, minority investment alliances—partnerships in which one firm takes a minority position in another company—help build long-term interests that cannot be realized by occasional top-level contacts.[37] The same strategy applies to firms trading ownership rights.

Singapore Airlines traded 3 percent of its capital base in return for about 5 percent of the shares of Delta Airlines of the United States. Both companies thereby achieved a variety of objectives: blending schedules at shared destinations, establishing joint operations and marketing, and generally cooperating for mutual benefit. Singapore Airlines also entered into a similar equity-swapping alliance with Swissair.[38]

For IBM, minority investment alliances have become a major strategy for operating in Western Europe. Between 1990 and 1992, IBM purchased equity stakes in 200 software and computer service companies.[39] IBM hopes that the long-term partnership implied by minority investment alliances will lead to more elaborate associations among its partners.

IBM's purchase of a minority stake in Groupe Bull, the French state-owned computer maker, characterizes the importance of such equity alliances. The original agreement provides Bull access to IBM's RISC-chip (reduced instruction set computing) technologies. In return, Bull supplies IBM with portable and notebook computers. The agreement also includes an arrangement to cooperate in a wide range of technical and commercial ventures. For instance, Bull agreed to make circuit boards for IBM, while IBM produces RISC products at manufacturing sites in France.[40]

Affiliations are associations in which partners take on similar identities or long-term objectives. In France, Alexander & Alexander owns 49.9 percent of the Societe Generale de Courtage d'Assurances, one of that nation's largest insurance brokers. In Germany, A&A acquired 20 percent each of two brokerage companies, Industrie-Assekuranz GmbH and Carl Jaspers Sohn, which then merged to form Jaspers Industrie Assekuranz GmbH. Deutsche Bank also has a 20 percent interest in the new company.

The firm used a similar approach in penetrating other European markets. Alexander & Alexander has a 49 percent interest in Ganat Alexander of Spain, as well as in Alexander & Mata of Portugal, and in A&A Sigorta of Turkey. Fides Alexander of Switzerland is another associate of A&A, in which the parent firm holds a 45 percent interest.[41]

Some U.S. firms have spun off operating divisions to form what may be termed "satellite enterprises." This new form of organization bears a resemblance to the *keiretsu* alliances found in the Japanese trading and industrial complexes. In 1991, IBM announced that it would become a federation of smaller companies hopefully better able to respond quickly to the changing demands of the marketplace.

In the future, IBM may own only a majority – or even just a minority – interest in some of the newly created companies that it hopes to establish. A unit's managers may be accountable to a different set of shareholders than the parent corporation's. Mature businesses may also be spun off.

IBM has already done this in the case of its Information Products Division in Lexington, Kentucky.[42] The stock of the new company, called Lexmark International, is owned by Clayton & Dubilier, IBM, and Lexmark employees. Lexmark and IBM continue to be strategically aligned through a host of agreements covering the printers and other "peripheral" equipment. These arrangements extend to the use of the IBM logo on many of the products Lexmark manufactures and markets. IBM is Lexmark's largest customer.

IBM sold its major interests in Lexmark because as an operating division Lexmark did not fit with the company's overall objective of being the preeminent computer systems company with multinational clients. Yet IBM recognized a continuing need for the printer made by Lexmark. Because the printer and personal computer sales are so closely intertwined, a continuing relationship with Lexmark was considered crucial. The negotiating process for the formation of this satellite enterprise was very different from the typical merger or acquisition. The negotiation was long, the style cooperative, and the discussion of price one of the last items on the agenda. The partnership concept was considered essential from the outset.[43]

The Decision to Enter into Equity Alliances

Although equity alliances are different from acquisitions, the factors a firm considers before participating in a joint equity swap, for instance, are not unlike those that arise in mergers or acquisitions. The motivation in swapping equity rather than merging companies, however, is more to ensure closer cooperation between particular parts of each organization than to engage in across-the-board collaboration. Perhaps of greatest importance, these alternative investment associations enable the individual companies to maintain their separate identities.

By trading the equity of member firms, partnerships are typically designed to be long term. AT&T acquired a 20 percent interest in Italtel, an Italian producer of telecommunications equipment, in exchange for a 20 percent interest in AT&T Network Systems International. The alliance was formed with the intention that each company cooperate to provide networking equipment not only in Italy but also in other European countries.

Ford's stakes in Mazda, the Japanese automaker, and Excel Industries, a window manufacturer, represent another example of the long-term, close associations typical of minority equity partnerships. On the one hand, Ford's association with Mazda is motivated by a need to maintain a cooperative tie with a strong Japanese auto producer. On the other hand, Ford and Excel's partnership is based on the buyer/supplier relationship between the two firms. Ford requires Excel's critical glass-shaping know-how early in the design process to ensure an optimal trade-off between glass-forming techniques and vehicle window designs. Excel seeks to retain a committed long-term buyer of its products.[44]

Firms generally do not engage in joint equity swaps if the partners do not have a clear, long-term strategy that benefits each firm substantially. Such an alliance is rarely effective between two traditional competitors.[45]

Conclusion

The nature of strategic alliances is complex, and a variety of organizational structures is used to create them. Many difficult issues have to be dealt with, such as the amount of equity invested by each partner, the scale and scope of cooperation, the duration of the arrangement, and so on. We have not attempted to develop an exhaustive representation of the way companies form and maintain relationships with other enterprises. The categories presented here should be useful in determining the issues that arise when firms cooperate, especially across national borders and in response to restrictive trade policies enacted by foreign governments.

In spite of the cooperative nature of most alliances, the resulting web of interrelationships between firms within specific industries can be viewed as an impediment to innovation and long-term economic efficiency. Dominant firms involved in a myriad of alliances with rivals may not have the incentive to innovate. The trend toward international partnerships and alliances could be used by firms and governments to freeze the structure of industry by means of a global market-sharing arrangement.[46] One widely held view maintains that the key to a competitive advantage is a firm's willingness to upgrade core skills, products, and process technologies rather than to rely too heavily on either contributions by the alliance partner or fruits of the alliance itself. Strong competition within an industry is fundamental to the incentive to innovate and to maintain a competitive advantage.[47]

Strategic alliances are not a guaranteed formula for successfully competing in either domestic or foreign markets. Many companies believe that alliances are necessary to reduce the risks associated with operating in an uncertain and fast-changing global marketplace. Yet the nature of alliances is essentially one of a trade-off between risk-sharing and innovation. Risk-sharing may help ensure that a company obtains or maintains a competitive position in the short run, but innovation and the ability to adapt to changes in the world market are far more important in determining a firm's position in the long run.

Business alliances are anything but easy. They require extreme clarity in regard to objectives, strategies, policies, relationships, and people. Alliances may become more problematic the more successful they are.[48] In a similar vein, one study of eight large successful U.S. companies concludes that joint ventures often seem unstable because they are continually in a state of evolutionary development. They create a heavy demand on management time and effort and require both partners to be tolerant of ambiguities.[49]

7

Summary and Conclusions

The range of business responses to the threats and opportunities in the international economy is expanding as rapidly as the global marketplace itself. As shown in table 7.1, each response is accompanied by important advantages and serious drawbacks.

The table does not show, however, the numerous linkages and interrelationships among the various options. For example, a direct investment in Mexico by an Asian firm may be part of a broader strategy for increasing exports to the United States. Cross-licensing a product among companies in different regional markets may be a preliminary step toward joint ownership within those areas. Long-term strategic alliances may be based on an array of earlier successful business relationships ranging from manufacturing subcontracting to technological cooperation.

The precise form of the interfirm relationship, including the interlinkages that may develop as the partnership develops over time, depends upon the specific strategies of the participating companies, as well as on the social, political, and institutional environment in which the firms find themselves. As we have attempted to show in this book, the factors and considerations a company must take into account are as complex as they are numerous.

This study does not attempt to present a precise blueprint that a firm's management can use to guide its decision making. We hope, nevertheless, that the analysis contained in the preceding chapters will be useful in helping companies to avoid the more obvious pitfalls. We also hope it will be of use to government policymakers, who often act without understanding the full impact of their actions on the private sector.

Business errors in attempting to develop a role in the international economy are not confined to the traditional shortcomings of approaches such as exporting and franchising. They also extend to the newer and currently popular strategic alliances in all of their varied forms. Regardless of which of these specific responses — or combination of them — the modern business firm selects, the consequences of responding to globalization can be profound for the individual company.

The basic composition of its work force can be altered fundamentally. Half of Xerox's 110,000 employees now work on foreign soil. Only half of Sony's employees are Japanese. Globalization also alters the composition of the firm's finances. More than half of Digital Equipment's revenues come from overseas operations. One-third of General Electric's profits are derived from its international activities.

One of the most striking examples of the global marketplace has been described by George Shultz, former U.S. secretary of state. He tells of a shipping label on integrated circuits made by a U.S. firm that read: "Made in one or more of the following countries: Korea, Hong Kong, Malaysia, Singapore, Taiwan, Mauritius, Thailand, Indonesia, Mexico, Philippines. The exact country of origin is unknown."

As we have seen, the choice among exporting, licensing, and entering into strategic alliances and other relationships with other business firms is often strongly influenced by governmental policies and practices. These may be actions by the nation in which the parent company is located and the country in which the firm is trying to develop a new presence. The governmental action may range from the support-

TABLE 7.1
Alternative Business Responses to the Global Marketplace

Alternatives	Characteristics	Advantages	Disadvantages
Direct strategies for marketing abroad	Exporting Turnkey operations	Expands markets Maintains control Maintains domestic production	Faces foreign barriers Sensitive to exchange rate fluctations
Cooperative contractual agreements	Licensing Franchising Subcontracting	Requires small investment Concentrates on core activities	Minimizes control
Wholly owned affiliates	Greenfield operations Mergers and acquisitions	Maintains full control Localizes production	Requires large investment May be unpopular politically

Strategic nonequity alliances	R&D cooperatives Technology swaps Joint production/ marketing agreements Informal alliances	Accesses markets Provides global presence Flexible Co-opts potential competitors Reduces risk	Exhibits uncertain control Slows down decision making Potentially unstable May lose technology to competitors
Strategic equity alliances	Joint ventures Joint equity swaps Affiliates Other investment alliances	Accesses new markets/ fields Minimizes risks Results in lower costs than direct investment	Requires complex, detailed contracts Often difficult to manage

Source: Center for the Study of American Business, Washington University.

ive, such as a tax incentive to invest in a specific region, to a barrier, notably restrictions on imports.

Table 7.2 outlines the major governmental barriers facing a company trying to do business in another country and shows how companies can overcome them. The reader should be cautioned, however, that companies also take into account many traditional business considerations in making these choices. These range from differences in production cost to limits to the firm's own financial capability. These private factors strongly influence, and frequently dominate, the decision to enter a national market as well as the method of entering it. Strategic alliances and other cooperative associations between companies are frequently the choice in high-tech, competitive markets. Wholly owned subsidiaries, on the other hand, are typical of stable markets and tend to be found where a much greater degree of product uniformity exists.

The variations of interfirm interactions we have noted may be ascribed to attempts to overcome barriers and reduce market risks, but other explanations have also been suggested. The motive for cooperating, the perceived direction of the alliance, and the technology and other resources brought to it by the partners will influence the specific form the alliance will take. For instance, equity partnerships are typically utilized when the form of cooperation entails the use of highly specific assets, such as the joint construction of a manufacturing facility. Equity partnerships allow greater control over the operation of such facilities because the contractual relationship in this case must be more formally delineated than when nonequity strategic alliances are formed.[1]

Although it is beyond the focus of the research underlying this book, it is useful to speculate as to the nature of the enterprise that is emerging in response to the pressures and opportunities of the global marketplace. A pertinent example is Asea Brown Boveri (ABB), the Swedish-Swiss transnational conglomerate. After combining separate Swedish and Swiss firms in 1987, ABB acquired or took minority

TABLE 7.2
Business Responses to Governmental Barriers

Barrier	Business Response
Trade Barriers Tariffs and quotas Domestic content restrictions Reciprocity rules Government procurement restrictions	Establish manufacturing operations in target country Acquire local firm Subcontract or purchase locally Develop products jointly Shift to higher-priced exports (for quotas)
Investment Barriers Limits on foreign ownership of local enterprises	Enter into joint ventures with local firms Give away nominal majority ownership Franchise local firms Enter into licensing agreements Set up R&D cooperation or technology swaps
Restrictions on repatriation of earnings Fear of expropriation	Set up affiliate or correspondent relationships with local firms Reinvest overseas
Regulatory and Tax Barriers In home country In foreign nations Informal foreign barriers	Shift high value-added activities to low-tax, low-regulation nations Market through local distributors

Source: Center for the Study of American Business, Washington University.

107

positions in approximately 60 companies in Europe, the United States, and elsewhere. Its major U.S. acquisitions include the power transmission and distribution business of Westinghouse, Cincinnati Milacron's industrial robotics business, and all of Combustion Engineering, a major manufacturer of power generating plants, furnaces, and process automation.

ABB is attempting to become a model of the "post-transnational" corporation. The company's management views it as a federation of enterprises spanning international borders to the point of appearing stateless, but at the same time it is so entrenched in local countries that it seems multi-domestic. Its eight corporate board members are from Sweden, Switzerland, Germany, Luxembourg, and the United States. English is the official language for all major deliberations. The financial records of its 5,000 major profit centers are kept in U.S. dollars.[2] ABB exemplifies the emerging global firm.

Many employees of private firms – and their governmental representatives – are not, however, happy with these globally oriented developments, especially when they seem to affect the prospect for jobs in their city, province, or county adversely. Their response is twofold: to try to restrict imports and often to restrain the export of technology. The response of the more internationally oriented firms is that economic incentives and technological progress know no national boundaries. Many foreign markets are expanding more rapidly than those in the older industrialized regions. The citizens of each nation can choose either to participate in the growing international economy (and receive both the benefits and the competitive threats) or crawl into their national shell and strive for greater self-sufficiency.

Not every company is going to make a grand success of it in the challenging international economy of the 1990s. Indeed, there will be winners and losers as business firms adjust to the threats and opportunities of the global marketplace. Nevertheless, we can learn something about the nature of the winners. A comprehensive survey by Booz-Allen in mid-1990 showed that the more fully "global" companies enjoyed far higher profit margins and greater returns on assets than either the purely domestic-oriented firms or those that exported from a domestic home base. Similarly, a study of the 1980s by the Conference Board concluded that multinationals grew faster than domestic firms.[3] The lesson: globally oriented firms will be more effective than enterprises limited to a single geographic market in overcoming the challenges of and successfully competing in a world marketplace. As globally oriented enterprises, they also will be less prone to call on government to restrict competition from "foreigners."

Notes

Chapter 1: Competing in a Global Marketplace

1. Yves Doz, "International Industries: Fragmentation Versus Globalization," in Bruce R. Guile and Harvey Brooks, eds., *Technology and Global Industry* (Washington, D.C.: National Academy Press, 1987), 115.

2. Raymond Vernon and Ethan Kapstein, "National Needs, Global Resources," *Daedalus* 120 (Fall 1991): 14.

3. J. Brian Quinn, "Globalization: A Research Base," *Tuck Today*, Summer 1991, p. 4.

4. Joseph Nemec, Jr., and Barbara A. Failer, *A Special Report on Globalization* (New York: Booz-Allen & Hamilton, 1991).

5. See Murray Weidenbaum, "The Business Response to the Global Marketplace," *Washington Quarterly* 15 (Winter 1992): 173.

6. Wilhelm Nolling, *Fortress Europa? The External Trade Policy of the European Communities* (Frankfurt, 1988), 31; *Basic Statistics of the Community*, 24th ed. (Luxembourg: Eurostat, 1987), 269.

7. "Pacific Rim Economies," *The World & I* (May 1991), 48.

8. Joseph S. Nye, Jr., "Sealing Global Fault Lines," *Christian Science Monitor*, August 8, 1991, p. 18.

9. Anthony P. Carnevale, *America and the New Economy* (Washington, D.C.: American Society for Training and Development and U.S. Department of Labor, 1991), 17–18.

10. Rudiger Dornbusch, "The Case for Trade Liberalization

in Developing Countries," *Journal of Economic Perspectives* 6 (Winter 1992): 69–85. For an interesting counterdiscussion, see Dani Rodrik, "The Limits of Trade Policy Reform in Developing Countries," *Journal of Economic Perspectives* 6 (Winter 1992): 87–105.

11. Carnevale, *America and the New Economy*, 18.

12. Nye, "Sealing Global Fault Lines," 18.

13. Carnevale, *America and the New Economy*, 18–19.

14. Heinz Riesenhuber, *Global Partnerships in Research and Technology* (Bonn: Konrad Adenauer Stiftung, 1991), 4–5.

15. Vernon and Kapstein, "National Needs, Global Resources," 15–16.

16. Other researchers have also adopted the distinction between equity and nonequity alliances. See, for instance, J. Peter Killing, "Understanding Alliances: The Role of Task and Organizational Complexity," in Farok J. Contractor and Peter Lorange, eds., *Cooperative Strategies in International Business* (Lexington, Mass.: D. C. Heath and Company, 1988), 56; Elisa B. Miller and Paul Surovell, "Co-Production in the USSR: Joint Production without Joint Ventures," *Columbia Journal of World Business* 23 (Summer 1988): 61–66; Gary P. Pisano, Michael V. Russo, and David J. Teece, "Joint Ventures and Collaborative Arrangements in the Telecommunications Equipment Industry," in David C. Mowery, ed., *International Collaborative Ventures in U.S. Manufacturing* (Cambridge, Mass.: Ballinger Publishing Company, 1988), 23–30. This distinction, however, may be blurred in reality. Nevertheless, it highlights important aspects of the cooperative nature of many strategic alliances.

Chapter 2: Marketing Abroad Directly

1. Ronald E. Yates, "U.S. Firms Told to Try Harder in Japan," *Chicago Tribune*, November 10, 1991.

2. Murray Weidenbaum, *Technology and Economic Performance: A Different View of the Federal Role* (St. Louis, Mo.: Washington University, Center for the Study of American Business, 1991), 1–2.

3. A product category must meet three requirements before the U.S. Bureau of the Census will classify it as "advanced technology": (1) the product must contain technology from "a recog-

nized high technology field," (2) it must represent "leading edge" technology in its field, and (3) the technology must constitute a "significant" part of the product. U.S. Bureau of the Census, *Trade in Advanced Technology Products*, SB-2-89 (Washington, D.C.: U.S. Bureau of the Census, August 1989), 2. The data are from the U.S. Bureau of the Census.

4. Dun & Bradstreet, *Comments on the Economy* 2, no. 4 (August/September 1991): 2.

5. Companies represented by the ABC are characterized as high-growth, mid-sized U.S. companies, whose average revenue typically grows at more than 20 percent a year. John S. McClenahen, "How U.S. Entrepreneurs Succeed in World Markets," *Industry Week*, May 2, 1988, p. 49.

6. Charles R. Taylor, *North America: The New Competitive Space* (New York: Conference Board, 1991), 9.

7. Bonnie Heineman Wolfe, "Finding the International Niche: A 'How To' for American Small Business," *Business Horizons* 32, no. 2 (March/April 1991): 13. The U.S. farm subsidy program reduces the competitiveness of American-produced honey because it keeps the price artificially high.

8. Candice Stevens, "Technoglobalism vs. Technonationalism: The Corporate Dilemma," *Columbia Journal of World Business* 25 (Fall 1990): 43.

9. See also figure 1.1.

10. McClenahen, "How U.S. Entrepreneurs Succeed," 48.

11. Mark Robichaux, "Enterprise: Focus of Exports," *Wall Street Journal*, June 26, 1991, p. B1.

12. Alan E. Branch, *Elements of Export Marketing and Management*, 2d ed. (London: Chapman and Hall, 1990), 3.

13. "Case Study: Marsh-McBirney, Inc.," *Economic Insights*, January/February 1991, p. 8.

14. Dun & Bradstreet, *Comments on the Economy*, 3.

15. Lawrence W. Tuller, *Going Global: New Opportunities for Growing Companies to Compete in World Markets* (Homewood, Ill.: Business One Irwin, 1991), 18.

16. Louis Uchitelle, "Small Companies Going Global," *New York Times*, November 27, 1989, p. 25.

17. Dun & Bradstreet, *Comments on the Economy*, 2.

18. "Marsh-McBirney," 8.

19. Michael Porter, *The Competitive Advantage of Nations* (New York: Free Press, 1990), 55–56.

20. Wolfe, "Finding the International Niche," 14.

21. Monci Jo Williams, "Rewriting the Export Rules," *Fortune*, April 23, 1990, p. 90.

22. Porter, *Competitive Advantage of Nations*, 56.

23. Ibid.

24. Uchitelle, "Small Companies Going Global," 25.

25. Dun & Bradstreet, *Comments on the Economy*, 2.

26. J. M. Livingstone, *The Internationalization of Business* (New York: St. Martin's Press, 1989), 88–89.

27. "Machine Builders Take Systems Responsibility," *Modern Plastics* 68 (March 1991): 76.

28. David Silbert, "Small Business Exporting: Success in Small Doses," *Canadian Business* 60 (October 1987): 17–18.

29. Livingstone, *Internationalization of Business*, 89.

30. The share of world trade attributed to exports from the United States is about 14 percent. World trade accounted for by all U.S. companies – including foreign subsidiaries and production facilities located in other countries – is approximately 17 percent. See Robert B. Reich, "The Trade Gap: Myths and Crocodile Tears," *New York Times*, February 12, 1988, p. 27.

Chapter 3: Cooperative Contractual Arrangements

1. Charles R. LaMantia, "A Connecticut Yankee in the Global Economy," *Chief Executive*, January/February 1989, p. 26.

2. Uchitelle, "Small Companies Going Global," 25.

3. Gordon Adams, *Arms Exports and the International Arms Industry* (Washington, D.C.: Defense Budget Project, December 1991), 10.

4. Stevens, "Technoglobalism vs. Technonationalism," 44; William H. Davidson, *Global Strategic Management* (New York: John Wiley & Sons, 1982), 52.

5. Udayan Gupta, "How Big Companies Are Joining Forces with Little Ones for Mutual Advantages," *Wall Street Journal*, February 25, 1991, p. B1.

6. Jim Impoco, "Fighting Japan on Its Home Turf," *U.S. News & World Report*, June 24, 1991, p. 50.

7. William A. Dymsza, "Success and Failure of Joint Ventures in Developing Countries: Lessons from Experience," in Contractor and Lorange, *Cooperative Strategies in International Business*, 408, 411–412.

8. Branch, *Elements of Export Marketing and Management*,

97–98; Ming-Je Tang and Chwo-Ming Joseph Yu, "Foreign Market Entry: Production-Related Strategies," *Management Science* 36 (April 1990): 476–489.

9. Franklin R. Root, "Entering International Markets," in Ingo Walter and Tracy Murray, eds., *Handbook of International Management* (New York: John Wiley & Sons, 1988), 2–15.

10. Branch, *Elements of Export Marketing and Management*, 96; Root, "Entering International Markets," 2–15.

11. Rick Whiting, "Japan Partners Its Way into Elusive Workstation Arena," *Electronic Business* 15 (September 4, 1989): 17–18.

12. Quoted in Ted Holden, with Joseph Weber and Peter Galuszka, "Who Says You Can't Break into Japan?" *Business Week*, October 16, 1989, p. 49.

13. Root, "Entering International Markets," 2–15; Branch, *Elements of Export Marketing and Management*, 96–97; Davidson, *Global Strategic Management*, 55–56.

14. Branch, *Elements of Export Marketing and Management*, 96–97; Davidson, *Global Strategic Management*, 55–56.

15. David C. Mowery, "Collaborative Ventures between U.S. and Foreign Manufacturing Firms: An Overview," in Mowery, *International Collaborative Ventures*, 7.

16. See Robert T. Keller and Ravi R. Chinta, "International Technology Transfer: Strategies for Success," *Academy of Management Executive* 4, no. 2 (1990): 37; Ben L. Kedia and Rabi S. Bhagat, "Cultural Constraints on Transfer of Technology across Nations: Implications for Research in International and Comparative Management," *Academy of Management Review* 13 (October 1988): 559–571.

17. Branch, *Elements of Export Marketing and Management*, 97–98; Philip Voss, Jr., "International Marketing Myopia," *Chief Executive*, January/February 1991, p. 33.

18. Stevens, "Technoglobalism vs. Technonationalism," 44.

19. Mowery, "Collaborative Ventures," 7.

20. Peter Burrows, "How Texas Instruments Attacks the Global Market," *Electronic Business* 17 (May 6, 1991): 34.

21. Henry Urrows and Elizabeth Urrows, "Kodak's Photo CD Promised for 1992," *Document Image Automation* 11, no. 2 (March/April 1991): 89–97.

22. Keller and Chinta, "International Technology Transfer," 36.

23. Ibid., 33.

24. Michael J. Hyland, "Successful Process Licensing: List-ing of Engineering and Construction Firms," *Chemical Engineering*, supplement (June 1991), 5–25.

25. Mowery, "Collaborative Ventures," 8.

26. Ibid., 7; Stevens, "Technoglobalism vs. Technonational-ism," 44.

27. Virginia Lopez and David Vadar, *The U.S. Aerospace Industry in the 1990s* (Washington, D.C.: Aerospace Industries Association, 1991), 21–22.

28. Peng S. Chan and Robert T. Justis, "Franchise Management in East Asia," *Academy of Management Executive* 4, no. 2 (1990): 75.

29. Lisa J. Moore, "The Flight to Franchising," *U.S. News & World Report*, June 10, 1991, p. 68.

30. Carnevale, *America and the New Economy*, 17–18.

31. George Gilder, "A New Breed: The Global Opportunists," *Success* 35 (September 1988): 40.

32. Frank Go and Julia Christensen, "Going Global," *Cornell Hotel and Restaurant Administrative Quarterly* 30, no. 3 (1989): 75.

33. John P. Hayes and Gregory Matusky, "Goodbye to the Small Fries . . . Hello to the Big Guys," *Inc.*, September 1989, p. 111.

34. Gilder, "New Breed," 41; Dennis Chaplin, "International Licensing: Master Plan," *Marketing*, October 20, 1988, pp. 29–30.

35. Go and Christensen, "Going Global," 74; Chaplin, "International Licensing," 29.

36. Chan and Justis, "Franchise Management," 77; Go and Christensen, "Going Global," 74.

37. Hayes and Matusky, "Goodbye to the Small Fries," 109–110.

38. Doug Finch, "Getting Big Building Small," *New England Business* 12 (September 1990): 76–78.

39. Gregory Matusky, "The Competitive Edge: How Franchises Are Teaching the Corporate Elephants to Dance," *Success* 37 (September 1990): 59.

40. See Bruce Walker, *A Comparison of International versus Domestic Expansion by U.S. Franchise Systems* (Tempe, Ariz.: International Franchise Association, June 1988); Go and Christensen, "Going Global," 76.

41. James B. Hayes, "Wanna Make a Deal in Moscow?" *Fortune*, October 22, 1990, pp. 113–115.

42. Chan and Justis, "Franchise Management," 81; Richard T. Ashman, "Born in the U.S.A.," *Nation's Business* 17 (November 1986): 41, 44.

43. Chan and Justis, "Franchise Management," 83.

44. Go and Christensen, "Going Global," 76.

45. Ibid., 77; Paul Meller, "Back to the USSR," *Marketing*, August 9, 1990, pp. 22–23.

46. Chan and Justis, "Franchise Management," 79; Tatsuya Anzai, "Kentucky Fried Chicken Japan: TSE-Listed KFCJ Holds a 90% Share of the Market," *Tokyo Business Today* 58 (October 1990): 56–58.

47. Chan and Justis, "Franchise Management," 79; Go and Christensen, "Going Global," 78.

48. See Masaaki Kotabe, "'Hollowing-out' of U.S. Multinationals and Their Global Competitiveness: An Intrafirm Perspective," *Journal of Business Research* 19 (August 1989): 2.

49. Michael Berger, "Exit Multinationals, Enter Strategic Alliances," *Billion*, June 1990, 17; Kevin Done, "Ford Signs Engine Deal with Yamaha," *Financial Times*, March 6, 1991, p. 5.

50. Kenichi Ohmae, "The Global Logic of Strategic Alliances," *Harvard Business Review* 67 (March/April 1989): 145.

51. Stevens, "Technoglobalism vs. Technonationalism," 43. See also Michael Radnor, "Technology Acquisition Strategies and Processes: A Reconsideration of the 'Make versus Buy' Decision," *International Journal of Technology Management* (1991), 113–135.

52. Laurence Hooper, "Big Blue Cultivates New Markets by Thinking Small," *Wall Street Journal*, February 27, 1991, p. B2.

53. Berger, "Exit Multinationals," 19.

54. Susan Helper, "How Much Has Really Changed between U.S. Automakers and Their Suppliers?" *Sloan Management Review* 32 (Summer 1991): 18.

55. Stevens, "Technoglobalism vs. Technonationalism," 43–44.

56. Gilder, "New Breed," 35–40.

57. Mark L. Fagan, "A Guide to Global Sourcing," *Journal of Business Strategy* 12 (March/April 1991): 21.

58. Ibid., 23; Livingstone, *Internationalization of Business*, 92.

59. Fagan, "Guide to Global Sourcing," 22; Helper, "How Much Has Really Changed?" 16–17.

60. Joseph L. Cavinato, "The Logistics of Contract Manufacturing," *International Journal of Physical Distribution & Materi-*

als Management 19, no. 1 (1989): 13–20; Jack Baranson, "The Essence of Transnational Alliances," *Industrial Management* 32 (March/April 1990): 31; Fagan, "Guide to Global Sourcing," 23.

61. Kotabe, "'Hollowing-out' of U.S. Multinationals," 2.

62. Baranson, "Essence of Transnational Alliances," 31.

63. G. Pascal Zachary, "U.S. Probes Japanese Companies on Charges of Withholding Parts," *Wall Street Journal*, January 16, 1991, p. B4.

64. Fagan, "Guide to Global Sourcing," 22–23.

Chapter 4: Building and Buying Overseas Operations

1. S. J. Kobrin, "Trends in Ownerships of American Manufacturing Subsidiaries in Developing Countries: An Inter-Industry Analysis," *Management International Review* 28, special issue (1988): 74–76.

2. Roy C. Smith and Ingo Walter, *The First European Merger Boom Has Begun* (St. Louis, Mo.: Washington University, Center for the Study of American Business, 1991), 3.

3. McClenahen, "How U.S. Entrepreneurs Succeed," 47–48. See also note 5 in chapter 2.

4. Louis Uchitelle, "U.S. Businesses Loosen Link to Mother Country," *New York Times*, May 21, 1989, p. 30.

5. David E. Sanger, "I.B.M. Concessions to Mexico," *New York Times*, July 25, 1985, p. D5.

6. Amy Borrus, with Wendy Zellner and William J. Holstein, "The Stateless Corporations," *Business Week*, May 14, 1990, p. 101.

7. Branch, *Elements of Export Marketing and Management*, 100–101.

8. "The Myth of Economic Sovereignty," *Economist*, June 23, 1990, p. 67.

9. Robert S. Eckley, *Global Competition in Capital Goods: An American Perspective* (New York: Quorum Books, 1991), 134–135.

10. Konji Ishizumi, *Acquiring Japanese Companies* (Oxford: Basil Blackwell, 1990), 17.

11. Ibid., 31–32.

12. Stevens, "Technoglobalism vs. Technonationalism," 43.

13. United Nations, *World Investment Report, 1991: The Tri-*

ad in Foreign Direct Investment (New York, United Nations, 1991), 3, 31.

14. Raymond J. Mataloni, Jr., "Capital Expenditures by Majority-Owned Foreign Affiliates of U.S. Companies, Latest Plans for 1991," *Survey of Current Business* 71 (March 1991): 26–33. Mahnaz Fahim-Nader, "Capital Expenditures by Majority-Owned Foreign Affiliates of U.S. Companies, Revised Estimates for 1991," *Survey of Current Business* 71 (September 1991): 32–38.

15. Murray Weidenbaum, *The New Wave of Business Regulation* (St. Louis, Mo.: Washington University, Center for the Study of American Business, 1990). See also Richard B. McKenzie and Dwight R. Lee, *Quicksilver Capital: How the Rapid Movement of Capital Has Changed the World* (New York: Free Press, 1991).

16. United Nations, *World Investment Report*, 39.

17. Ibid., 26–27.

18. See Benjamin Gomes-Casseres, "Firm Ownership Preferences and Host Government Restrictions: An Integrated Approach," *Journal of International Business Studies* 21, first quarter (1990): 1–22.

19. Benjamin Gomes-Casseres, "Joint Venture Instability: Is It a Problem?" *Columbia Journal of World Business* 22 (Summer 1987): 97–102.

20. Robert B. Reich, "Japan Inc., U.S.A.," *New Republic*, November 26, 1984, pp. 19–23.

21. F. J. Contractor and P. Lorange, "Competition vs. Cooperation: A Benefit/Cost Framework for Choosing between Fully Owned Investments and Cooperative Relationships," *Management International Review* 28, special issue (1988): 10.

22. Daniel Pearl, "Federal Express Plans to Trim Assets in Europe," *Wall Street Journal*, March 17, 1992, p. A3.

23. Martin K. Starr, *Global Corporate Alliances and the Competitive Edge: Strategies and Tactics for Management* (New York: Quorum Books, 1991), 141.

24. Smith and Walter, *First European Merger Boom*, 3.

25. Douglas Lamont, *Winning Worldwide: Strategies for Dominating Global Markets* (Homewood, Ill.: Business One Irwin, 1991), 181–182.

26. Davidson, *Global Strategic Management*, 59–63.

27. Starr, *Global Corporate Alliances*, 143.

28. Jordan Lewis, *Partnerships for Profit: Structuring and Managing Strategic Alliances* (New York: Free Press, 1990), 16–

17; Benjamin Gomes-Casseres, "Ownership Structures of Foreign Subsidiaries: Theory and Evidence," *Journal of Economic Behavior and Organization* 11, no. 1 (1989): 8.

29. Gomes-Casseres, "Ownership Structures," 8–9.

30. Lewis, *Partnerships for Profit*, 16, 299.

31. Thomas A. Leipzig, "A 1990s Twist: Cross-Border Deals Are Thriving in the Middle Market," *Review* 36, no. 1 (1992): 35.

Chapter 5: Strategic Alliances
without Equity Investment

1. Lewis, *Partnerships for Profit*, 1.

2. David Lei, "Strategies for Global Competition," *Long Range Planning* 22, no. 1 (1989): 104.

3. For alternative characterizations of strategic alliances, see Peter Lorange and Johan Roos, *Strategic Alliances: Formation, Implementation and Evolution* (Cambridge, Mass.: Blackwell Publishers, 1992); Farok Contractor and Peter Lorange, "Why Should Firms Cooperate? The Strategy and Economic Basis for Cooperative Ventures," in Contractor and Lorange, *Cooperative Strategies in International Business*, 3–30.

4. Robert McGough, "The Grand Alliance," *Financial World*, December 10, 1991, p. 40.

5. Ibid., 46.

6. "U.S.-Japan Chip Deal," *New York Times*, September 2, 1991, p. 18.

7. Randall Smith, "Southwestern Bell, 2 Others Win Right to Acquire 51% Voting Stake in Telemex," *Wall Street Journal*, December 10, 1990, p. A3.

8. Robin Gareiss, "Carriers Set Global Plan," *Communications Week*, June 3, 1991, p. 3.

9. Jonathan B. Levine and John A. Byrne, "Corporate Odd Couples," *Business Week*, July 21, 1986, p. 100.

10. Godfrey Devlin and Mark Bleackley, "Strategic Alliances: Guidelines for Success," *Long Range Planning* 25, no. 5 (1988): 18.

11. Pisano, Russo, and Teece, "Joint Ventures and Collaborative Arrangements," in Mowery, *International Collaborative Ventures*, 23.

12. Berger, "Exit Multinationals," 15.

13. Bruce Stokes, "Come Fly with Me," *National Journal*, March 31, 1990, pp. 778–783; Berger, "Exit Multinationals," 15.

14. Quoted in Carol J. Loomis, "Can John Akers Save IBM?" *Fortune*, July 15, 1991, p. 42.

15. Joseph L. Badaracco, Jr., *The Knowledge Link: How Firms Compete through Strategic Alliances* (Boston, Mass.: Harvard Business School Press, 1991), 6.

16. Kenichi Ohmae, *The Borderless World* (New York: Harper Collins, 1990), 131.

17. Badaracco, *Knowledge Link*, 62.

18. Tuller, *Going Global*, 290.

19. The sole exception to date is Batam Island, in which an export-processing zone is being established. Foreign companies locating in that area may set up wholly owned subsidiaries. Enterprises operating in the zone will get full exemption from import duties, such as on raw materials used in products to be exported. See Sara Khalile, "Market Opportunity: Indonesia," *International Business*, November 1991, pp. 26–27.

20. Peter Lorange and Johan Roos, "Why Some Strategic Alliances Succeed and Others Fail," *Journal of Business Strategy* 12 (January/February 1991): 27.

21. "UPS Using Alliances to Gain Worldwide Growth," *St. Louis Post-Dispatch*, November 29, 1991, p. 5E.

22. Theodore Moran and David Mowery, "Aerospace," *Daedalus* 120 (Fall 1991): 140–141.

23. Badaracco, *Knowledge Link*, 13–15.

24. Michael Blumenthal, "Macroeconomic Policy," in Martin Feldstein, ed., *International Economic Cooperation* (Cambridge, Mass.: National Bureau of Economic Research, 1987), 16.

25. Lorange and Roos, "Why Some Strategic Alliances Succeed," 25.

26. Ellen Goldbaum, "New Alliances Share the Work and the Rewards," *Chemical Week*, December 7, 1988, p. 36.

27. Lewis, *Partnerships for Profit*, 18; Mowery, "Collaborative Ventures," 10.

28. James B. Treece and Karen Lowry Miller, "The Partners: Surprise! Ford and Mazda Have Built a Strong Team: Here's How," *Business Week*, February 10, 1992, p. 104.

29. Ohmae, *Borderless World*, 120.

30. Henry J. Crouse, "The Power of Partnerships," *Journal of Business Strategy* 12 (November/December 1991): 8.

31. Lei, "Strategies for Global Competition," 103; Farok J. Contractor, "Contractual and Cooperative Modes of International Business," *Management International Review* 30, no. 1 (1990): 49.

32. Robert Manis, "Searle Expanding Presence in Japan," *St. Louis Post-Dispatch*, September 6, 1991, p. C1.

33. Lewis, *Partnerships for Profit*, 4.

34. Gomes-Casseres, "Joint Venture Instability," 97–102.

35. Philippe de Woot, *High Technology Europe: Strategic Issues for Global Competitiveness* (Oxford: Basil Blackwell, 1990), 85.

36. Lorange and Roos, "Why Some Strategic Alliances Succeed," 26; Mowery, "Collaborative Ventures," 11.

37. Rosabeth Moss Kanter, "Transcending Business Boundaries: 12,000 World Managers View Change," *Harvard Business Review* 69 (May–June 1991): 162.

38. Valerie Rice, "Why Teaming Up Is So Hard to Do," *Electronic Business* 17 (April 8, 1991): 30–34; Starr, *Global Corporate Alliances*, 138.

39. Quoted in David Whiteside and James B. Treece, "Corporate Odd Couples," *Business Week*, July 21, 1986, p. 104.

40. Clyde Prestowitz, *Trading Places* (New York: Basic Books, 1989): 5–72.

41. Karen J. Hladik, "R&D and International Joint Ventures," in Contractor and Lorange, *Cooperative Strategies in International Business*, 187.

42. David E. Sanger, "Japan Wary as U.S. Science Comes Begging," *New York Times*, October 27, 1991, p. E16.

43. John Hagedoorn, "Organizational Modes of Inter-firm Cooperation and Technology Transfer," *Technovation* 10, no. 1 (1990): 17–30.

44. Robert Brainard, "Internationalism R&D," *OECD Observer*, no. 174 (February/March 1992): 9.

45. Jacob M. Schlesinger, "AT&T, NEC Agree to Cooperate on Basic Chip-Making Technology," *Wall Street Journal*, April 23, 1991, p. B4.

46. Lei, "Strategies for Global Competition," 102.

47. Robert Simison and Stephen D. Moore, "Volvo Defends Alliance with Renault, Saying the Logic Will Soon Be Evident," *Wall Street Journal*, June 17, 1991, p. A7.

48. Richard L. Hudson, "Digital and Olivetti Plan to Collabo-

rate on Research Project at British Facility," *Wall Street Journal*, June 17, 1991, p. A5A.

49. Thomas C. Hayes, "Texas Instruments to Work with Hitachi," *New York Times*, November 21, 1991, p. C4.

50. "High Speed Plane Requires Global Alliances," *R & D Magazine*, December 1991, p. 50.

51. Hladik, "R & D and International Joint Ventures," 189.

52. Stevens, "Technoglobalism vs. Technonationalism," 44; Hladik, "R & D and International Joint Ventures," 188.

53. Mowery, "Collaborative Ventures," 11.

54. Steven Schlossstein, *Asia's New Little Dragons* (Chicago: Contemporary Books, 1991): 306.

55. Stevens, "Technoglobalism vs. Technonationalism," 44.

56. Hladik, "R & D and International Joint Ventures," 189–190.

57. David C. Mowery, "Joint Ventures in the U.S. Commercial Aircraft Industry," in Mowery, *International Collaborative Ventures*, 71–110.

58. Hladik, "R & D and International Joint Ventures," 192.

59. Ibid., 194.

60. Dori Jones Yang, "Boeing Knocks Down the Wall between the Dreamers and the Doers," *Business Week*, October 28, 1991, p. 121.

61. Miller and Surovell, "Co-Production in the USSR," 61.

62. Crouse, "Power of Partnerships," 5.

63. John D. Morrocco, "Korean Air Negotiates Agreement to Coproduce Sikorsky UH-60," *Aviation Week & Space Technology* 130, no. 24 (June 12, 1989): 225–227; David F. Bond, "Korea Picks F/A-18 for Coproduction, Cites Capabilities, Industry Benefits," *Aviation Week & Space Technology* 132, no. 1 (January 1, 1990): 34–35.

64. Ohmae, *Borderless World*, 125–126.

65. *A & A World*, second quarter, 1990, p. 3.

66. Miller and Surovell, "Co-Production in the USSR," 65.

67. Devlin and Bleackley, "Strategic Alliances," 18.

68. Lewis, *Partnerships for Profit*, 92.

69. Kahan Hakansson and Jan Johanson, "Formal and Informal Cooperation Strategies in International Networks," in Contractor and Lorange, *Cooperative Strategies in International Business*, 368–379.

70. Lewis, *Partnerships for Profit*, 92, 232.

71. Roger F. Roberts, "Competition and Cooperation," a paper presented at the World Trade Association, Irvine, Calif., September 27, 1991, p. 3.

Chapter 6: Strategic Alliances with Equity Investment

1. Christopher A. Sawyer, "The Global Village: Major Players and Their Partners," *Autoweek*, January 28, 1991, pp. 20-21; "Car Industry Joint Ventures: Spot the Difference," *Economist*, February 24, 1990, p. 74.

2. "Foreign Investment Moves into East Europe," *Christian Science Monitor*, October 16, 1991, p. 13; "Gerber Moves into Poland," *New York Times*, October 4, 1991, p. C3; "Dow Chemical in Czech Deal," *New York Times*, November 6, 1991, p. 19; Pauline Yoshihashi, "Chevron Signs Initial Pact to Develop the Tengiz Oil Field in Kazakhstan," *Wall Street Journal*, May 8, 1992, p. B2.

3. "Coca Cola Sets Russia Venture," *New York Times*, January 17, 1992, p. C3.

4. Steven Greenhouse, "Seeking to Give a New Life to a Dying Soviet Industry," *New York Times*, December 23, 1991, p. C1ff.

5. Conference Board, *Global Presence and Competitiveness of U.S. Manufacturers*, Report no. 977 (New York, 1991), 20.

6. Tuller, *Going Global*, 60-78.

7. Lopez and Vadar, *The U.S. Aerospace Industry in the 1990s*, 26-28.

8. Benjamin Gomes-Casseres, "Joint Ventures in the Face of Global Competition," *Sloan Management Review* 30 (Spring 1989): 17-26.

9. Damon Darlin and Joseph B. White, "GM Venture in Korea Nears End," *Wall Street Journal*, January 16, 1992, pp. 1ff.

10. Louis Uchitelle, "Hunting for Riches in Ex-Soviet Lands," *New York Times*, December 27, 1991, pp. A1, A9.

11. "G.E.-Tungsian Venture in Hungary Hits Snags," *New York Times*, March 28, 1992, p. 17.

12. Willem T. M. Koot, "Underlying Dilemmas in the Management of International Joint Ventures," in Contractor and Lorange, *Cooperative Strategies in International Business*, 347-367; D. Robert Webster, "International Joint Ventures with Pacific Rim Partners," *Business Horizons*, March/April 1989, p. 67.

13. Hercules has since sold its interest in Himont to Montedison.

14. "Aerospace Offset Venture Nears Takeoff," *New York Times*, September 23, 1991, p. C13.

15. "Deere to Join Venture with Fiat and Hitachi," *New York Times*, November 7, 1991, p. C3.

16. Howard W. French, "GTE-Led Group Wins Venezuela Phone Stake," *New York Times*, November 16, 1991, p. 19.

17. Stephen Engelberg, "GM Venture to Build Opel Cars in Poland," *New York Times*, February 29, 1992, p. 17.

18. John J. Kelly, "World-Wide Warriors," *Wall Street Journal*, October 4, 1991, p. R4.

19. Robert L. Simison, "Babes in Europeland," *Wall Street Journal*, October 4, 1991, p. R5.

20. Anthony Ramirez, "IBM Link with British Telecom Set," *New York Times*, October 8, 1991, p. C4.

21. Derek Kent-Smith, "The European Company's Ability to Compete in a Global Marketplace," *Journal for Corporate Growth* 7, no. 2 (1989): 19–22.

22. Kathryn Rudie Harrigan, *Managing for Joint Venture Success* (Lexington, Mass.: Lexington Books, 1986), 7; idem, "Strategic Alliances: Their New Role in the Global Competition," *Columbia Journal of World Business* 22 (1987): 67–69.

23. Mark Casson, *Enterprise and Competitiveness: A Systems View of International Business* (Oxford: Clarendon Press, 1990), 153.

24. Starr, *Global Corporate Alliances*, 148.

25. Gomes-Casseres, "Joint Ventures in the Face of Global Competition," 17–26; Contractor and Lorange, "Why Should Firms Cooperate?" 3–30.

26. Starr, *Global Corporate Alliances*, 148.

27. Gomes-Casseres, "Joint Venture Instability," 97–102.

28. "The Soviet Disunion: What's Happening Now That the Party Is Over?" *Process* 3, no. 1 (1992): 5.

29. Ford S. Worthy, "Keys to Japanese Success in Asia," *Fortune*, October 7, 1991, p. 158.

30. Gomes-Casseres, "Joint Venture Instability," 100–101.

31. Contractor and Lorange, "Why Should Firms Cooperate?" 12; Erin Anderson and Barton Weitz, "Forging a Strategic Distribution Alliance," *Chief Executive*, November/December 1991, p. 73.

32. Gomes-Casseres, "Joint Ventures in the Face of Global

Competition," 21–22; "Europe's Companies after 1992: Don't Collaborate, Compete," *Economist*, June 9, 1990, pp. 17–19.

33. Alan I. Murray and Caren Siehl, *Joint Ventures and Other Alliances: Creating a Successful Cooperative Linkage* (Morristown, N.J.: Financial Executives Research Foundation, 1989), 28.

34. Starr, *Global Corporate Alliances*, 154.

35. de Woot, *High Technology Europe*, 119.

36. Joel Bleeke and David Ernst, "The Way to Win in Cross-Border Alliances," *Harvard Business Review* 69 (November–December 1991): 127–135.

37. Lewis, *Partnerships for Profit*, 232.

38. Michael Westlake, "The Mating Planes," *Far Eastern Economic Review* 147, no. 7 (February 15, 1990): 37.

39. Jonathan B. Levine, "Look Who's Helping Defend Fortress Europe," *Business Week*, February 17, 1992, p. 131.

40. Roger Cohen, "IBM to Invest $100 million in Groupe Bull," *New York Times*, January 29, 1992, pp. C1, C6.

41. *A&A World*, second quarter 1990, pp. 1–3.

42. John Markoff, "IBM Announces a Sweeping Shift in Its Structure," *New York Times*, November 27, 1991, p. 1.

43. Peter D. Goodson, "The Innovative Characteristics of Future Transactions," *Journal for Corporate Growth* 7, no. 2 (1991): 38–42.

44. Lewis, *Partnerships for Profit*, 111.

45. Ibid., 232–233.

46. Moran and Mowery, "Aerospace," 151.

47. Porter, *Competitive Advantage of Nations*.

48. Peter Drucker, "The Futures That Have Happened Already," *Boardroom Reports*, December 15, 1989, p. 8.

49. Peter Lorange, "Cooperative Strategies: Experiences of Some U.S. Corporations," in Paul Shrivastava and Robert B. Lamb, eds., *Advances in Strategic Management*, vol. 6 (Greenwich, Conn.: JAI Press, 1990), 27–28.

Chapter 7: Summary and Conclusions

1. The discussion is illustrative of the transaction cost economics approach. See, for instance, Oliver C. Williamson, *The Economic Institutions of Capitalism: Firms, Markets and Relational Contracting* (New York: Free Press, 1985); Benjamin Klein, Robert G. Crawford, and Armen A. Alchian, "Vertical Integration,

Appropriable Rents, and the Competitive Contracting Process," *Journal of Law and Economics* 21 (October 1978): 297–326.

2. Ted Agres, "Asea Brown Boveri – A Model for Global Management," *R & D Magazine*, December 1991, pp. 30–34.

3. Nemec and Failer, *Special Report on Globalization*, 11; Conference Board, *Global Presence and Competitiveness of U.S. Manufacturers.*

Index